DEL
IN SYRIA & IRAQ

STEVE STONE

PROLOGUE

Syria 2014

On July 4, 2014, it was just after midnight on Independence Day when a series of air strikes by U.S. aircraft were launched against an Islamic State camp known as "Osama bin Laden Camp." As the bombs dropped twelve Delta operators and Jordanian Special Forces parachuted from Black Hawk Stealth Helicopters like the ones used in Operation Neptune Spear. These Black Hawk 'stealth helicopters' had a much lower radar and heat signature. They are also virtually noiseless. Perfect for a more clandestine approach. The only downside is the extra weight from all the modifications. Which means they cannot fly as high as the standard Black Hawk or Pave Hawk helicopters. The Delta Operators all looked down into a derelict and empty compound. It looked as though Islamic State had abandoned it. The main gate to the prison was wide open as were the doors that the operators could see. Some of the windows were broken and the courtyard was overgrown with weeds and brush. The ground was littered with rubble and garbage. They could almost smell the place from the chopper. It smelled like an overflowing trash can.

The Delta and Jordanian Special Forces jumped into the cool night air. The Islamic State prison they were jumping into was believed to be holding several high value prisoners including the captured American reporter James Foley. The prison not a proper prison just a makeshift prison located within an oil refinery about 11 miles south east of Raqqa in Syria. As soon as they landed the U.S. and Jordanian Special Forces blocked off the only main road towards Ar-Raqqah before beginning their assault on the prison. The twelve operators had to fight all the way into the prison against quite stiff resistance. They were assisted by several Jordanian Special Forces guys as well. Sadly, on searching the prison no prisoners were found and it looked they had only just been moved. It would later turn out that the prisoners had been moved about 24 hours earlier.

Delta operators then decided to conduct a dangerous but necessary house to house search in Uqayrishah in the vain hope the prisoners

5

may have been hidden there. This was to prove futile. Whilst searching, Islamic State reinforcements from Ar-Raqqah arrived. It was not long before Delta and the Jordanians soon became pinned down by an aggressive force. The firefight raged for nearly three hours with a mixture of small arms and RPG fie.

Rounds were bouncing off the walls and the ground as Delta and the Jordanian Special Forces returned fire. This firefight proved how deadly Islamic State could be when properly co-ordinated and with the necessary manpower.

American aircraft were also fired upon with RPGs but thankfully not one was successful in hitting any of the aircraft trying to aid the Delta Operators on the ground. With no sign of the hostages and an intense firefight that had already injured one Delta operator and one Jordanian special forces guy. It was decided to make a tactical retreat. By 0300 hours it was all over and several buildings had been severely damaged in the raid. Islamic State had lost eight fighters including trainee IS leaders from Tunisia and Saudi Arabia.

ONE - CROSSHAIR

Afghanistan 2010

"Live by chance, love by choice, kill by profession"

Looking down the scope of my sniper rifle I could see all the way into the village, mothers scooped up their children and ran indoors. I felt like I was on the set of a Western movie when the bad guy comes to town. It was a typical Afghan village made up of small and large compounds with dusty tracks instead of roads. To a westerner, they looked so basic, but were functional and suited the climate very well. The streets were now deserted and a deathlike silence smothered the village. U.S. Rangers in two Humvees pushed forwards towards the Village part of an operation to capture a Taliban local commander. Intelligence had placed him in one of the larger compounds towards the far edge of the village.

Delta Force has been operating in Afghanistan since the war began in 2001. Delta took part in the battle for Tora Bora at the start of the War in Afghanistan in 2001. Tora Bora was a vertical no man's land in the mountains of Afghanistan close to the Pakistan border. Those that were there said it was almost like being in hell - with its enormous jagged snow-covered ridge lines and high peaks separated by deep ravines and valleys studded with mines. Delta helped guide in various jet fighters such as the F-15 and F-16s along with variants of the C-130 to bomb al-Qaeda almost into submission including dropping a BLU-82B "Daisycutter" bomb. Sadly, even with the presence of Delta and the SBS, bin-Laden managed to slip away across the border into Pakistan. The mountainous area was hard to fully contain and the mujahideen assisting us did not like to fight at night. However, al-Queda's mountain base was destroyed and bin-Laden would be finally killed by Seal Team Six during Operation Neptune Spear in 2011. For us not to get given the bin-Laden op was a bitter pill to swallow after how close we came to capturing bin-Laden in 2001.

Back in Afghanistan, my job was to act as overwatch and protect the team. I had moved into position earlier on in the day slowly wilting under the hot sun. Two Delta Operators from my team had decided to inset themselves into the Ranger unit proceeding up the road. My job was to take out any potential threat before it had a chance to kill any of the guys. The Taliban were extremely sneaky and their tactics was to often lure coalition forces into an ambush or a trap. This was week four of my tour of duty in Afghanistan having come almost straight from an overseas operation. I was part of B Squadron, Delta. Our job was to assist conventional forces in removal of various pockets of resistance and the targeting of key Taliban personnel. I joined the 'Unit' as an Operator after passing selection nearly three years ago. The selection was the easy part – the steep learning curve and two years of constant training had been intense.

I was two floors up on a compound roof with a commanding view of the main road into and out of the village. A light breeze whipped up small swirls of dust from the roof that kept on misting up the scope slightly. My radio burst into life to tell me the Rangers were approaching the edge of the village. I stared down my scope even more intensely watching for any movement which may turn into a threat. The Humvees filled my scope as I followed them in. They screeched to a halt becoming enveloped in a large cloud of dust. Eight Ranges leapt out, two of them I recognised as Delta Operators from my team, Craig and Marc who were helping to support the operation.

They moved forwards hugging the sides of the buildings on a high state of alert looking for signs of IEDs and any potential threat. I trained my scope just ahead of them also looking for any potential threat. Almost out of nowhere a figure dressed in black appeared and raised his AK-47 directly at the advancing soldiers. His body now filled my crosshairs and I gently squeezed the trigger of my Barrett M107. I could feel the recoil from the weapon through my entire body as the 107 let out a round. I had been holding my sights on the chest of the young male. I rocked back with the recoil, he disappeared from my crosshair. A killing shot drops a man so fast it seems like the earth just swallows him up. When I came back to rest again, the only hint that just an instant before a man had been standing there was a faint cloud of atomized blood and tissue momentarily suspended in the air.

The M107 is a .50 caliber, shoulder fired, semi-automatic sniper rifle. It has enough power to go straight through an engine block. It will pretty much obliterate any human being who finds themselves in the path of one of its rounds. It has also proved useful in destroying IEDs at a distance. It is good for a target up to around 2 miles depending on conditions.

When the M107 is fired, the barrel initially recoils for a short distance, while being securely locked by the rotating bolt. After the short travel the bolt is engaged via a post on the bolt in the curved cam track in the receiver. This then turns the bolt to unlock it from the barrel. As soon as the bolt unlocks, the accelerator arm strikes it back, transferring part of the recoil energy of the barrel to the bolt to achieve reliable cycling. The barrel stops and the bolt continues back, to extract and eject the spent case. Finally, a new cartridge is fed from the box magazine and placed into the chamber before finally being locked into to the barrel. The weapon at the same time is cocked ready to fire its next round.

The Taliban fighter lay dead, blood pouring out of what was left of his chest. This was my fifth kill as a sniper. I cannot say I feel any real remorse or guilt. I try to see the enemy as a target that must be eliminated. If not, American soldiers will die.

There is more to being a sniper than just being a good shot. The best shots are not necessarily the best snipers. Just because you can hit a target does not mean you can spot the target in the first place. I am not the best shot by a long way, but better than average at spotting a target. You must be able to study your terrain and surroundings. In training, you are taught to see things you previously missed such as discerning subtle shapes, noticing the smallest amount of movement. You must train yourself to not only be an excellent observer but to keep your observation skills at the highest possible level.

The Rangers continued forward along with the two Delta operators who had positioned themselves at the back playing 'tail end Charlie' protecting the rear flanks. I took a deep breath realising I had saved them from being injured or killed. The Taliban wanted all of us dead no matter what the cost was. They hated being occupied by any forces and for whatever reason the American forces seemed hated more than any other coalition force. This was my second tour in Afghanistan the first tour was as an Army Ranger in 2004. Not that much has changed in those six years, Afghanistan is still unstable and trying to find its feet. The government has yet to gain full control and offer its people security. Even in 2016 the Taliban are slowly creeping back into power and causing a real headache for the Afghan government. We are still there along with other special forces trying to help train the Afghan Army and undertake reconnaissance missions. As well as prevent the Taliban slowly creeping back into power.

As the Rangers edged ever closer to the Taliban compound, I could hear more doors closing and the sound of blinds being drawn. No one wanted to get involved, fearing reprisals from the Taliban. Out of the corner of my eye I noticed another black clad figure appear on the roof, this time he was carrying a RPG (Rocket Propelled Grenade) and about to fire. An RPG is designed to fragment into hundreds of shards of razor-sharp steel, which are blasted forward from the point of the explosion, fanning out and tearing flesh or light armour to shreds. RPG rounds can be set to either airburst mode going off after a set distance mid-air or explode on impact in detonating mode. The Taliban has used airburst mode to bring down helicopters by setting the RPGs to explode close enough for the shrapnel to shred hydraulic lines and electrical wiring looms.

I moved my crosshairs onto his central body mass, as I did so, rounds started to impact about ten feet from my location. They knew where I was – I was in as much danger as the Rangers making their way up the street. I had to take out the RPG first, then quickly move. I fired and the round found its target. The Taliban fighter was blown apart by the round. The RPG clattered to the ground next to the body parts of the deceased Taliban fighter.

I quickly packed up as yet another volley of fire hit the compound roof, as I slung my M107 onto my back and picked up my M4. I made my way down the stairs of the compound and out onto the street. My M4 was pressed firmly into my shoulders and I pointed it in whatever direction I looked, seeking out any potential target. As soon as I had found a suitable location I radioed in a situation report and requested fire support from an Apache. I could no longer see the eight Rangers, but with Taliban fighters up high. An Apache was the best bet to locate and neutralize them.

Within minutes a single Apache was on station, its distinctive rotor roar could be heard even when it was a couple of miles out. More than likely alerting the Taliban to its presence. It scanned the roof tops and surrounding area and found nothing. The guys in the Apaches gave a couple of rooftops a volley of 30mm cannon fire. Ranger reinforcements were just a few minutes out, and I had to help sweep the high ground. The Rangers would come in and do a proper sweep of the village. As soon as the Rangers arrived the Apache had to leave to go on another mission in Helmand. On arrival in the village the Rangers began to sweep through the village when a Hilux pick-up truck appeared with a DShK mounted on the back. Typical Taliban armor. The Hilux made a very fast and strong platform to mount a variety of weapons on. Islamic State have used the same tactics in Syria and Iraq. The Rangers quickly opened fire on it with two 90-millimeter recoilless rifles and it was quickly put out of action. It was obvious that the Taliban had sent in reinforcements and it was getting more dangerous by the second.

Finally, the team got to the compound and knocked on the door; there was no answer, so they kicked the door in. On entering, they found a family inside. A man along with his wife and three young children. As the team burst in the whole family started to scream and shriek. In the very few words of Pashto that Marc knew he said that they were American soldiers and were not here to hurt them. They calmed down a little when Marc asked if the Taliban had been here. They replied no. We knew they had been here but the family was too afraid of reprisals from the Taliban to say anything. The team undertook a search of the compound but found nothing. The Taliban had not left any trace that they had been staying here.

They had obviously either fled or found a new place to hide. More than likely using fear to force a villager to take them in. To try and search each building would take a large amount of resources and do more harm than good. The mission was a partial success, we had picked up some local intelligence and killed another two Taliban fighters. The local commander we had hoped to capture had fled – which was a disappointment to us all. But, that was all part of the cat and mouse game we played with the Taliban.

The important tactical operational lessons learnt by Delta in Mogadishu were put into practice during Operation Enduring Freedom. The Taliban and al-Queda would also come away learning that U.S. military was not as weak as bin-Laden had said in an interview. When he said that the American withdrawal from Somalia proved that America was far weaker than the Soviet Union who fought in Afghanistan for years. Even the numerous precision bombing missions in the Middle East and Africa did nothing to change his point of view. Al-Qaeda and the Taliban worked together and supplied the base in the Tora Bora Mountains that they though would be invincible. They soon found out the hard way America was far from weak and would retaliate with a knockout blow. A quote which I will never forget being told in Afghanistan from the early part of the war. *"Don't piss in the wind, don't sword fight with Zorro, and do not piss off the United States of America and George Bush!"*

TWO – STRESS PHASE

In the autumn of 2006, I found myself with 119 officers and sergeants at a secret and remote camp for my selection to see if I was worthy of joining Delta. I had already been through numerous pre-tryout psychological and physical tests. For the next month, I would stay in a camp surrounded in steep hills and mountains in the North-East area of the United States.

I was already a sergeant in the Rangers and most of those I was with were also from the Rangers. All I had to do was to make it through the next month without an injury or quitting to make it into Delta. The odds were stacked against me, by the end of the month most of the fine officers and sergeant's I was with would be gone. At most, only one in five of us would pass the tough selection process. The first three weeks were hard. It is hard for anyone who has not been through a selection process for Special Forces to understand how hard it is. You are pushed beyond what you think are you own mental and physical limits. Those that cannot exceed their limits fail. Then there are those unlucky few who pick up an injury through no fault of their own.

Most Delta operators come from either the Rangers or Special Forces community. The basic grounding and skills required to be an operator are learnt before joining the Unit. These shooting, moving and communication skills form the basic mould that operator training builds on. There are those that have come from some bizarre places in the Army such as intelligence, computer whizz or even a linguist. Although, those types are rare, but the ones which make it through often bring a different type of intellect and individuality. This speaks volumes about a fair selection process that is said to be as secret as the Coca-Cola recipe!

I had the final navigation exercise to pass and I was through the stress phase. With only a handful of us left huddled together on a truck. We waited to be called forward into the dark night and be set off on our assigned route. We were all mentally and physically exhausted, but knew this was it. Pass this and we were through to the main training phase.

If we got the route right it would be around forty miles of dense vegetation, forest and mountain trails go up and down. You needed to find the quickest and best route to keep within the set time limits. The time limit was unknown to everyone but select training officers. We did not even know what time we had to beat. I was second to last out of the seven remaining out of the 119 who started twenty-five days ago. At just past 2200 hours I set off into the moonless night after having been given a set of short but precise instructions. I was equipped with a fake weapon, compass, maps and a sixty-pound rucksack. Snaking my way up a mountain path, I caught up with another candidate at the first rendezvous point who had managed to drop his map and was scurrying around in the dark trying to locate it. I felt absolutely shattered and had to dig deep for an energy reserve to keep going. I knew I was so near to passing, but it felt so far away. I now had a steep hill to climb further zapping me of precious energy. I set off trying to keep a good pace and the next couple of rendezvous points seemed to pass with ease. I had been going for twelve hours and guessed I must only have a couple of hours to go. My feet burned from the pain of old and new blisters. I had to just shut the pain off and keep going. I was by now totally disorientated having had to move up and over and then back down through low cloud cover. It had begun to rain heavily and my rain soaked kit added to the weight I had to carry. It also added to my misery as I was now tired, wet and cold. I headed to the next rendezvous point and I noticed a truck was parked up. I did not really have the time to take it in as had to make myself ready for my next rendezvous point. Out of the blackness an officer suddenly appeared and offered me his hand. "Congratulations, you have passed the stress phase of selection." I could not really take it in at first and thought it was just another part of the test to see if I would give up at being told I had passed. He insisted I had passed and finally it dawned on me I had done it. I cannot describe the feeling of elation. I knew I had many to pass something that better soldiers than me had failed.

All that lay ahead now was the final four days of testing mainly physiological and then a final, commander's board which I had to pass to be accepted into Delta. The final interview was with a board including the current commander of Delta. This was his chance to probe and prod at anything and every part of my past life. It included tours of duty, command decisions and the rationale for what I had done and why. The questions seemed endless. I knew I had to keep my cool and just answer them as best I could. For some unknown reason, I enjoy interviews and don't find it stressful. Give me a written test and I fall to pieces.

After being ushered out of the door and ushered back in, I was finally told I had passed. Although, to be classed as a fully functional Delta Operator, I still had six months of training ahead of me. These six months of operator training was perhaps the most interesting and eye opening time during my army career. I turned up to Fort Bragg on my first day of training for some of the toughest training in the world. This multi-million-dollar facility was built in the early 1980s to support the war on terrorism. The training facility is made up of two buildings one which is two storeys and the other a three storey building. It as areas for heliborn insertions. There are also various open air and enclosed ranges that I would use to train and home my skills on. As I parked up I remember looking up to see an MH-6 Little Bird swoop over come to a hover and see two operators fast rope down to the ground.

The course had been designed to take my existing skills and build on them along with enhancing them to a level I never thought I would reach. I was also here to be taught the dark art of counterterrorism. Which has always been the Unit's prime mission. To be able to undertake a counter terrorist operation require intensive training and a very high level of teamwork. This is all part of the six month operators course I was on. Once these skills have been taught it is our job as an individual to keep them razor sharp by intense and regular training.

Everything is taught from entry and exit to rappelling into buildings, aircraft and boats of various sizes. Use of stun grenades, lock picking and of course Delta's signature CBQ.

I learnt how to shoot and kill at a level I never thought possible. I learnt covert commando skills as well as how to centre a whole range of aircraft types, boats and buildings. Both the selection and training is not too dissimilar to the British SAS. Seeing as Delta was originally based on the SAS by our founder Charlie Beckwith. It was during Beckwith's time as an exchange officer with the SAS that he saw their capability and realized the U.S. needed a similar force. His idea was rejected on several occasions before finally being accepted. Delta came into being in November 1977. It was setup as a counter-terrorist unit. The Units focus was initially on hostage rescue along with covert operations and specialized reconnaissance. Delta is now known for its ability to plan and the amazing marksmanship of its operators.

A Delta Operator is very much at the centre of the Unit. Our needs and welfare come first. Each of us represent a sizeable investment in both time and money getting us trained to the required standard. It is said it costs nearly as much to train a Delta Operator as it does a jet fighter pilot. A typical sergeant will stay with the Unit for eight to twelve years passing on mission knowledge and know how. Failures are turned into success simply from what is learnt and passed on to successive generations of Delta operators. Our senior officers have spent years with the Unit, maybe ten or more and again build on knowledge and use past experience to put together workable plans. All of us know we have reached the highest achievement possible in the military even though it still feels as though Delta are treated as the underdogs in the Special Forces community. But, each one of us is intuitively a winner.

David Hunt a retired U.S. Army colonel in his book, 'They Just Don't Get,' it summed up a Unit operator:

Here is the recipe for Delta. You start with an already spectacular soldier who has a proven service record of say, five years, usually as part of Special Forces or as a Ranger. He volunteers to go to the mountains of West Virginia, where he must run 30 miles over mountains with over sixty pounds on his back plus his weapon. He must pass a series of mental and physical tests. Only one in fifty will make it through this process. Once you make it through this "selection," you then spend almost a year learning the "deadly arts" in a training program that is designed for masochists. And there you have it, a Delta warrior! These guys shoot 50,000 rounds of ammunition a year per man. They train in tunnels, in sewers, on high wires, and even in trees. They actually run with 60 to 100 pounds on their backs. They jump from airplanes carrying more than 500 pounds. These super soldiers can do amazing things.

The most important skill a Delta Operator has, is the ability to shoot to kill and make every bullet count. We are the superior predators and had to be far superior to those we would be taking on. During initial training I was taught on a wide range of weapons, both long and short barrelled weapons. The longer barrelled weapons included sniper weapons. Those that were excellent at sniping, were later given more extensive and intensive training to become the designated sniper within a team. The first three weeks of the course were spent on a rifle range sharpening up our skills and taking on board tips from various experts. My marksmanship skills took a leap forward and I felt like a killer ready to take on any terrorist. I could walk and shoot whilst still making highly accurate shots. We then moved on to shooting in teams of three and four blasting off. Delta operators begin their career in an assault troop. The more experienced and skilled operators can get assigned to a reconnaissance troop. The smallest unit is a four-man team. Four or five teams and a small HQ make up a troop.

THREE – WHAT A STATE

Iraq 2015

No one could have predicted we would be back in Iraq. By the beginning of 2016 there was nearly 5,000 American soldiers in Iraq. Some say we should have seen it coming. After the main forces left following the second Iraq war, Iraq was far from stable. With various factions fighting each other. Removing Saddam Hussein had left a power vacuum and a weak government. Islamic State also known as ISIS saw their opportunity to land grab and of course seize the precious oil wells which would act as a funding stream for them. Under Operation Inherent Resolve commanded by Lt. General Sean MacFarland. American air and ground forces are back in a limited number to try to support Iraqi security forces in getting rid of this new and quite worrying threat.

Islamic State are the greatest terrorist threat the world has ever known. These individuals are totally insane, their indoctrinated self-belief means they do not fear death, merely embrace it. They think nothing of killing anyone who will not follow their way of life. They will even kill their own if they do not toe the line or dare to speak out. Islamic State, like al-Qaeda, are classed as an Islamic fundamentalist group with Islamic fundamentalist beliefs and goals. They are advocates of the return of Muslims to the fundamental tenets of Islam, calls for the liberation of Muslims through the return to pure Islam and the creation of an Islamic state, called the caliphate. Islamic State sees pure Islam and an Islamic State as the only way to get rid of the problems faced by Muslims around the world.

Islamic State, emerged from radical Sunni jihadists in Iraq who fought under the banner "al-Qaeda in Iraq." Since 2004 their goal has been to create a caliphate - a hard line Islamic state crossing over the borders of Syria and Iraq. The single most important factor in Islamic State's rapid expansion has been the conflict between Iraqi Shias and Iraqi Sunnis. Most Iraqis are Shias. However ex-dictator Saddam Hussein was a Sunni and the absolute power of his Ba'ath party gave Sunnis the belief that they are the real majority and legitimate rulers. The difference between the two largest Muslim groups originated with a controversy over who got to take power after the Prophet Muhammad's death in 632AD. Abu Bakr was chosen as caliph, but a minority of Muslims favoured another man, Ali. Ali's followers became known as Shiat Ali, partisans of Ali – Shias. In 656, Ali became the fourth caliph after Abu Bakr was assassinated. Some Muslims, the ancestors of today's Sunnis, rebelled against him. Ali himself was assassinated in 661 after violence spread.

Islamic State have also been called ISIL (Islamic State of Iraq and the Levant) and ISIS (Islamic State of Iraq and Syria). Then on June 29, 2014, Islamic State announced the establishment of a new caliphate - meaning succession, and the group formally changed its name to Islamic State, often referred to as IS. Islamic State have a self-proclaimed status for religious authority over all Muslims across the world. They wish to bring Muslim inhabited regions around the world under its political control and sharia law. Starting with Iraq, Syria and territory in the Levant region, which includes Jordan, Israel, Palestine, Lebanon, Cyprus and an area in southern Turkey that includes Hatay. In 2012, sensing an opportunity, Abu Bakr al-Baghdadi Islamic State's leader dispatched some foot soldiers to join the fighting against Bashar al-Assad's government in Syria. In 2013, he announced that the group was merging with Jabhat al-Nusra, the other al-Qaida affiliate in Syria, to form a new group called the Islamic State in Iraq and al-Sham. Nusra, predominantly Syrian in membership, is more focused on the overthrow of Assad, whereas Islamic State is more international and interested in expanding its territory and enforcing Sharia law. Abu Bakr al-Baghdadi is our current top target and remains quite elusive and a high priority target.

This was not the first time Delta had been to Iraq, operators had taken part in both of the Gulf Wars and the subsequent search for Saddam Hussein. The first Gulf War saw Delta hunting down Scud missiles alongside the SAS in an area of operations called Scud Boulevard. The second Gulf War was the liberation of Iraq and the subsequent hunt for the leaders of the Saddam Hussein regime. We were also there to aid Iraqi forces in the quelling of terrorist forces trying to wrangle control of parts of Iraq.

Some of the guy's I was with, like myself had been to Iraq before and they would prove good sources of intelligence. Their knowledge of not only the terrain but the local people would help greatly. Delta has been back in Iraq along with the SAS, SBS and SEALs since 2014. With the odd mission meant Special Forces 'popping' into Syria and more recently Libya. Although, Syrian and Libyan missions were kept top secret for fear of political repercussions. In Iraq, we have helped to train up the Iraqi Army, undertake surveillance and even perform the odd takedown mission. Snipers like myself have been heavily used to take out key personnel at a distance.

Islamic State are well equipped with the usual DShK-38 12.7mm heavy machine guns, various mortar tubes, RPGs, PKMs and AK-47s. On top of these various American weapons including the M-16 have been captured from Iraqi forces as they advanced through Iraq. They have even captured the formidable M1 Abrahams tank. Although Islamic states don't have the technical knowhow nor parts to service them. They have been destroyed by us once located.

On our arrival in Iraq in April 2015. We were quickly deployed and I found myself in a Desert Patrol Vehicle (DPV). These dune buggies made from a steel frame with a VW engine on the back looked like they had come from an arcade game. They had been based on a typical Baja racer. Equipped with a .50 cal and a Mk-19 Grenade launcher they were quite potent as well. With an M60 mounted on the rear for flank protection. I won't say they are exactly fast. Once loaded up with all our kit and ammunition they make decent enough progress though.

We drove through the desert until we came upon an Iraqi Army base and rested there for a couple of hours before setting off again. We were headed towards the area around Mosul an Islamic State stronghold. Amongst the long stretches of wilderness, there was also small towns and settlements dotted around. We decided to skirt round them rather than go through. Observing what was going on. Our mission was to locate where enemy strongpoints were and make a note of locations and enemy strength. Any high ground we found offered us a more commanding view to survey a larger area. Islamic State did send out the odd patrol but they were more focused on trying to keep what they had whilst trying to creeping forwards further into Iraq. We had neither the ammunition nor the firepower to get into a large scale firefight. But, enough to protect ourselves.

We had one contact during our day's operation when some IS fighters started to engage us from about 200 yards away. Evil green tracer rounds tore up the ground in front of us. I fired the .50 cal changing to the 60 as we sped off into the desert. By the end of the day we had travelled hundreds of miles and picked out various Islamic State bases and strongholds. We rested up for a few hours until nightfall before heading back to our operations base and the usual debrief as to what we had seen. This would then be passed on to the CIA and Iraqi Security forces to aid in their operations. Our job was to help train and support and even accompany the Peshmerga on various operations. Peshmerga means "one who confronts death" or "one who faces death". "Pesh" means to stand in front of while "merga" means death.

Our specialist skills were still required though. Either for hostage rescue or capturing a key figure the Pesh would be used as fire support, if used at all depending on the mission. I like the other operators preferred taking Islamic State head on, one on one. Although we felt they were a dumbass group. Islamic State should never be underestimated their resolve and tenacity is second to none. Their weakness is blind faith and lack of training in some areas.

It was dark by the time we made it across the torturous desert and onto an asphalt road which enabled us to pick up the pace and head home avoiding any form of contact.

Once back at base we went through the usual 'hot wash.' These often have a mixture of CIA and Special Forces personnel. Including intelligence analysts, JSOC and anyone else invoked in the operation including 160th pilots if they had been involved.

The 160th were born out of Delta's first failed mission Operation Desert Claw. Out of its failure came both The Army Special

Operations Aviation Group. That organization was initially known as Task Force 160 and eventually evolved into the 160th Special Operations Aviation Regiment now known as the 'Night Stalkers' of today. They are one badass aviation outfit, able to operate at night and in al weather conditions anywhere in the world. They are the best at what they do and are absolutely the most courageous bunch of flyers you will ever find. The second was the Joint Special Operations Command (JSOC) that could pull together and oversee the Special Operations efforts of the various services. JSOC was soon instituted, but its command only had jurisdiction over counterterrorist operations.

The so called hot wash is run by a senior NCO. A hot wash is very similar to the U.S. Army's after action review. We use them to identify what went well and what went wrong. Also, looking at points to improve on as every operation is considered a learning opportunity. One part of the hot wash is that if you messed up, you knew about it, regardless of rank.

Once the first hot wash was completed we then have a second 'internal' hot wash. In this hot wash everyone is expected to pony up to any mistake no matter how small – it would be discussed. If anyone tried to cover it up, you can bet another operator would bring it up. The idea was that regardless of rank you can improve your performance by evaluating it. It required a thick skin and open mind at times but the process works. As soon as we finished the hot wash it was off to get some hot chow from the world's grumpiest chef.

A week later eight of us did found ourselves in a fearsome firefight just outside a small settlement that had around fifteen IS fighters occupying it. Once they opened up they never seemed to stop. A small wall next to my head exploded in a cloud of dust and debris as a steady stream of bullets flew just a few inches above my head. I lay flat on the ground returning fire as best as I could. I then started to crawl as fast as I could, eventually reaching better cover where I could get a better rate of fire down directly onto the advancing IS fighters. We fought them for a couple of hours and as dawn broke their guns fell silent. We had killed twelve, one lay wounded and two had decided to flee. We all slumped down outside our backs propped up on a brick wall. Exhausted and battle weary with a few superficial cuts and nicks we had survived. These Islamic State nutjobs could sure fight. What must be realised is that Islamic State wants to engage troops on the ground. The recent attacks have been to try and force countries to deploy troops by causing a massive outcry. It is as if they have something to prove not just to themselves but to the whole world that they can take on the west. Such is their self-belief - they are sure they would win as well. However, as the war against Islamic State has gathered momentum and the coalition has not just reduced Islamic State numbers but gradually pushed them back and areas have successfully been reclaimed. This has had the effect of encouraging more and more Sunni tribesmen to abandon Islamic State or encourage them to defy Islamic State by joining Sunni Mobilization Forces such as Hashd ash-Shaabi. Iraqi high command is still a bit of a problem but again coalition forces have helped train and prove that Iraqi forces can successfully take on Islamic State. This has also helped the coalition to have a greater say in which Iraqi commands are entrusted to lead key ground operations. However, the Iraqi Army has been partly rebuilt, and those units retrained and re-equipped by the coalition are performing noticeably better than the others. While the coalition's military power is slowly building, the increasing pressure on Islamic State is diminishing its capacity to resist.

FOUR - OPERATION

To do the job we do means sacrifices, both physical and mental. Notwithstanding the long periods of time away from home and loved ones. I have a wife and two young children and it does break my heart to leave them for such long periods. I miss seeing them grow up day by day and my wife at times feels like a single parent. There will come a time when I will no longer get sent off to foreign lands and get time to spend with my family. It is another life choice and I know it is a hard one for my family. They have the constant worry and fear of me being in harm's way. Retirement is still a few years away. I have the option to become part of the training team which would see me spending much more time closer to home.

I'm no different to anyone else. I just happen to have decided to fight for my country and in doing so found myself in some pretty badass situations. I get told how exciting it must be. I don't see it personally. I think it is more sheer terror than excitement at times. You never join up thinking you will become a killer or kill someone. Most join up for the challenge and be part of something. The comradeship and brotherhood is another element that you won't find in any other occupation, where your life literally depends on the actions of another.

In Iraq, we seemed to be getting a few more capture type raids. Intelligence would give us an individual and a location and we would go out and 'snag' them. Most of the time the raid went well. On the odd occasion, it did not quite go according to plan. On one particular occasion I was coming back down off a rooftop after playing overwatch on a snag operation. We had got in and out without firing a round. As I got to the bottom of the stairs I heard the familiar sound of numerous AK-47s going off, followed by the more worrying call over the radio that we had a man down. The rest of the team were pinned down and trying to fire back. I ran down a side street trying to find a good spot to get up high. I heard an explosion as an IS fighter threw a grenade not too far from my location. I had no idea if it had been aimed at me or someone else. But, I was not going to hang about to find out. I climbed on a roof top across from where the firefight still raged. I quickly set up my MK-14 EBR-RI rifle and got on with the business of hunting for a target. An IS fighter had just appeared with a belt fed weapon and he would be my first target. I got a shot straight through his head and saw the back of his skull blow off before he dropped like a stone to the floor. More IS fighters were coming down the street and I quickly fired a succession of rounds to halt them in their tracks. The rest of my team was still firing back, but still pinned down. I needed to get them some room to manoeuvre otherwise they were all screwed. Bullets were cracking through the air, some ricocheting off the walls in a series of small sparks. Marc and Craig started to get some serious fire down, knowing they were both outnumbered and outgunned. Marc knew he could not continue to stay in his current position and would need to move. The fighting continued as Marc and Craig ensure they conserved ammunition as they did not have a good line of sight on the enemy.

The other IS fighters were firing from round a corner and I could not get a good line of sight on them. My only option was to expose my position and move, literally jumping from one building to the next. Looking back, a totally stupid thing to do. In the heat of battle, you have to make split second decisions. Sometimes good, sometimes bad. But, my gamble paid off and after landing badly with my Mk-14 clattering to the ground. I quickly picked myself up and got into a position to fire. The Mk-14 EBR-RI is 7.62 mm sniper rifle has a standard weight 22.0" barrel and lugged GI flash hider; it is not to be confused with the Mk 14 Mod 0 or Mod 1.

To become a Unit sniper, I had to attend a sniper course. The Army course I was on, only had a pass rate of 50 percent, so yet again I knew I was going to have to work hard. I hopped my existing skills would aid passing the course though and give me the edge I needed. The course would last a total of ten weeks and was broken down into three phases. Phase one started with PFT (Physical Fitness Test) with a few failing it. Those that failed the PFT were sent packing without a second chance.

After the PFT we were put into pairs with one acting as a spotter whilst the other fired. Our snipper rifle was the M-40 or Remington

700 bolt action. Mounted on the top of the rifle was a x10 sniper scope. The scope had to be adjusted each time I went to fire. This was done by adjusting the bullet drop compensator to ensure the bullet hit the target the scope was pointing at. The spotter's job was to approximate wind speed as well as keep eyes on the target.

Phase two saw us undertaking more shooting and improving our estimation of distances and hitting targets accurately. We had to maintain a 70 percent average over three weeks just to stay on the course. As well as the actual shooting element of the training we also had to learn about concealment, which included making our own ghillie suits.

The only way to perfect a ghillie suit was to lay down in different environments and get your buddy to see if he could spot you. You then changed the colours and material on the suit until you became invisible. It was very much a trial and error process. Trying to break up your shape and blend in with the vegetation around you. With ghillie suits perfected, we started to learn and practice stalking, this saw the highest dropout rate of the course. We had to adapt and change our camouflage to different environments to remain concealed. Stalking is an art form and the last half a mile to the target the most important. You have to crawl low to the ground very carefully and at a slow speed. Ensuring you don't leave a trail. We had between three to four hours to stalk around a mile. An observer in an Observation Post would be watching out for us. If we were spotted before we got to 200 yards within the OP it would be a fail. Once at the 200-yard point we had to set up our scope and fire off a blank round. It was hot work with all our gear and a ghillie suit on.

The final Phase was Advanced Field Skills and Mission Employment including a final operation to prove all our newly acquired skills. The final three-day operation was a pass or fail for the entire course. We had to operate in pairs without any guidance or orders, just like we would have to in the field. We had to conceal ourselves in an OP. In the OP we took a note of everything which happened, before finally having to make a shot. Miss this shot and your failed sniper school –

this meant the pressure was well and truly on me to perform. I gently squeezed the trigger and hit the target exactly on the bull's eye. I had passed and could graduate from sniper school.

I was just able to get the right-hand side of one IS fighter in my crosshairs. I let off a round which sent the IS fighter's AK-47 flying into the air as he was pushed backwards by the force of the impact. Craig then managed to hit another IS fighter in the shoulder. This was enough for the rest of the team to be able to get up and run at full pelt down the street with bullets nipping at their heels as they did so. I soon followed in hot pursuit. Before looping back to where the IS Commander was. He was dead, having been shot by his own guys accidentally in the firefight. A bullet had ploughed completely through his leg, coming to rest just under the skin on the top of his thigh, missing the femur but hitting the femoral artery and he quickly bled to death. Other than grabbing his cell phone he was left where he had fallen. I then ran as fast as I could back to our rides. Almost leaping through the vehicle window throwing what I had collected onto the back seat before we sped off with rounds still impacting close by. Within a few minutes, we were out of danger and could slow the pace down. We all took a deep breath and gave a sigh of relief. It had been a close call and we could have so easily been overrun. We had got out with just a few scratches from the odd small shrapnel wound.

Had it been a much larger force, equipped with heavier weapons it could have meant a very different outcome. You try not to dwell on the "what if" you focus on the outcome, do your job and get another successful operation under your belt. Sometimes operations go according to plan other times unforeseen events happen that completely change the plan you had. It requires a commander who can think on their feet and make decisions in real time whilst undertaking an assault to keep an operation a success.

FIVE - SAAYAF

Syria May 2015

A counterterrorist operation has several distinct phases. The first is getting to the area of operations. At the same time, real time intelligence is gathered and analyzed by various agencies involved in the operation this continues until the operation is complete. After the raid intelligence is gathered and further analyzed. In Iraq, it has mainly been the American CIA, British Mi6 and Iraqi security forces who have gathered most intelligence although other organisations have been involved. Those individuals connected or part of Islamic State and subject to surveillance and capture by other countries such as France and Belgium have added in helping build a bigger picture of Islamic State and how it operates. Preventing several planned attacks in the process.

Once in operations we need to prepare, this could be target surveillance, checking of inner and outer security rings, enemy assets and any likely reinforcements. We then must discuss everything as an assault team and decided best approaches that we are all in agreement with. Tasks are allocated to the various specialists within the team, such as sniper, demolitions, tactical driver and so on. Finally, we undertake the assault, takedown of the objective and once completed a swift withdrawal was essential especially on an operation deep behind enemy lines.

Delta was down to take part joint operation with our British SAS cousins in Eastern Syria. They may speak the strangest version of English I have ever heard. But, the SAS are bloody good at what they do. The operation we had been tasked for was to take out Abu Sayyaf a top Islamic State financier. Sayyaf was a Tunisian who the government wanted to question about the terror group's financing. It was Sayyaf who set up a system where private buyers would line up with trucks at oil fields, pay in cash for crude oil, and transport it in their own trucks. The truckers would then sell this crude oil at a profit to local, makeshift refineries. This fuel once refined was then sold onto either roadside pumping stations or smugglers who would sell it onto more populated areas.

Sayyaf also wanted so that he could be questioned about hostages murdered by Islamic State including Kayla Mueller currently the last known American captive. Sayyaf was given custody of the American aid worker Kayla Mueller in September 2014 after she had suffered being Islamic State leader Abu Bakr al-Baghdadi's sex slave.

It was also hoped if captured he could be brought to justice and face terrorism charges. JSOC had been tracking Sayyaf since early 2014 due to his importance to Islamic State. The mission had originally been due to be undertaken in March 2015, but poor weather and intelligence issues had delayed it.

The SAS had been sent out to perform reconnaissance on our target several days before. To ensure the SAS participation was kept secret due to the usual political bullshit. They wore American uniforms and carried American weapons to keep their participation secret. They were even flow in by a U.S. V-22 Osprey tilt rotor aircraft. These ungainly looking aircraft with their oversized twin rotors and tilt wing design have become excellent workhorse now its reliability issues have been overcome.

In cities like Raqqa, Syria, where Islamic State is has established its headquarters, people are killed, tortured, detained, and oppressed to ensure they follow Islamic State Doctrine. These victims are not foreigners, but fellow Muslims whom the group has labelled apostates for not adhering to Islamic Sates religious laws. If a man is found drinking or a woman is not correctly veiled they are he beaten. The city has many of its building painted black and Islamic State flags hang all over the city. Earning it the dubious name of "Black Province."

Heavily armed checkpoints control passage into and out of the city. At theses checkpoints people are interrogated and inspected. Anyone who is thought to be a traitor which includes members of rival groups such as Nusrah Front or the Free Syrian Army (FSA). They are arrested and taken away. The streets are patrolled by IS fighters to ensure their laws are met this includes entering homes and schools to check women are correctly veiled. Anyone living there is living under a harsh regime and one reason so many have decided to leave Syria and Iraq seeking a safer country to migrate to. In Iraq those that have connections to the Saddam regime are still given a hard time and they too have found themselves needing to leave Iraq to find safety. The war against Islamic State has displaced millions of people and caused a mass migration to Europe. Hopefully, long term with Islamic State gone some may decide to return home and help re-build the country. After all that is a big part of what the coalition is doing in Iraq, trying to make its people safe from tyranny and persecution.

The Landing Zone for the raid was in Deir ez-Zor governorate. From here the SAS had to hike to their reconnaissance area close to the compound that Sayyaf was staying at. Once in a heavily camouflaged position. They used night vision goggles and a telescope to observe the target. As they got into their routine and fed back vital intelligence which would help us finalize the raid on Sayyaf. They monitored all movements into and out of the compound noting down timings and the numbers of 'Tangos' or hostiles believed to be at the compound. The most important part was to ensure Sayyaf was at the location and we got to him before he moved on.

As the planning stage of the forthcoming operation drew to its conclusion. It was the responsibility of each and every operator to ensure they knew the plan and got any thoughts, comments or questions ready for the briefback. The briefback is basically a final briefing on how each operator will carry out his duties once at the target. This is pretty much standard operating procedure within the Special Forces community. The briefback covered everything from the execution, support requirements, command structure, latest intelligence on the target, numbers of hostiles and any enemy positions within our area of operations. Finally, a concise and detailed narrative of what each operative would do in order to complete our objective. We wanted Sayyaf alive if at all possible to see if we could get any intelligence from him. However, we knew this was highly unlikely as these Islamic State nutjobs loved to fight and by killing them they believed they would become a martyr.

Once we had completed our briefback this was passed onto our commander so he knew we were ready to go. Our commander also knew exactly what we would require to execute the mission. With a plan in place it was time for our own individual equipment preparations ensuring our weapons and equipment was ready to deploy.

The plan was for the compound to be strafed by F-18 Super Hornets to help soften the target and blow a hole in the side of the building before we moved in. The SAS would help direct the F-18s onto their target as we made our way to the compound in helicopters carrying a total of fifteen Delta Operators, all hungry to get stuck in and do what we are trained to do. The adrenalin rush as you get close to the target is unreal. We launched our raid from Ain al Assad Air Base in Western Anbar Province with a flight time of one hour and fifteen minutes. The Iraqi government had been informed of the raid.

The plan was for the Pave Hawks to offload us close to the compound and then cover our entrance with rockets and 7.62 miniguns to try to quell any resistance.

The first available F-18 dropped its payload which fell slightly short. A second F-18 repeated the bombing run and scored a direct hit.

The ground beneath me flashed by over the desert as our bird neared the target. Fast and low was the best way to avoid be caught by any radar. There's nothing else that gives you as much of an adrenalin rush as making assault by helicopter. The doors of the chopper are taken off and you sit with your feet inside otherwise at full speed you would get yanked out of the Pave Hawk. The whine of the rotors along with the roar of the engines as ground rushes below. There is a pounding rush of air pouring over you tugging at your clothes making you feel like a cavalryman on horseback heading into battle. You race towards the target at a relentless pace once that is still the most exhilarating part of an operation. As the Pave Hawk slowed we slid our feet and legs over the edge of the chopper's floor ready to jump off as soon as we landed.

I was hanging my head out the doorway trying to see ahead through the dust kicked up by the rotors.

As I stepped off the chopper a cool breeze hit me, the sky was full of stars and presented a beautiful sight. One Pave Hawk took a few rounds on the ground but was still able to carry on with the attack. We moved forward as covertly as we could before all hell broke loose as the Pave Hawks opened up on the compound. Even with rockets and miniguns we were still taking fire and had to fight I way forward. One operator managed to hit an IS fighter firing his AK-47 straight at us. He fell straight off the roof and hit the ground with a hollow thud. After entering the compound through the hole created by the F-18. We split up into teams and all took different quarters of the large compound. It was a case of fighting through each room. For some elements of the team this meant hand to hand fighting. The hardest part was avoiding shooting any women and children which the Islamic State had decided to use as human shields. A so called 'double tap' to the head dropped the IS fighter without civilian loss. It was a scene of mayhem but not too dissimilar to a hostage rescue. A scenario we constantly trained for and the whole reason Delta Force came into being.

Marc and I took the lead in our team and pushed forward firing as we went. In the dark you could see the muzzle flashes from mainly AK-47s firing at us. But, I could also hear the distinctive sound of M16s being fired at us. We moved along the corridor which had doors on both sides. As we got just a few feet down the corridor an IS fighter suddenly appeared from behind a door. He was shot in the head and killed before he had time to lift his AK-47 up. In other areas of the compound Delta operators were in a fierce firefight with ISIS fighters who fought tenaciously and were much better trained than we had expected. It was a slow raid by our standards. But, when you end up undertaking room by room clearance as well as searching for IEDs or booby traps it always slows down progress.

Marc had a heavy build which end helped him become the Wrestling State champion. He was a natural born hunter. He had grown up with a family of hunters. He never stopped undertaking some form of fitness training. He spent virtually every day in the gym. With biceps the size of a cannon balls. His strength and agility would make a top athlete feel unfit. When back home in the States he would be up in the early hours prowling the local area tracking deer.

Finally, after hour an hour the compound was secure. When Sayyaf was found, he tried to grab a handgun and he was shot in the chest twice. We had killed fifteen IS fighters, which included Sayyaf. The loss of Sayyaf would be a blow to Islamic State and another one of their key personnel taken out. With the compound secure the SAS moved up and acted as a cutoff for any fighters trying to flee. Without a doubt, a few had fled the moment the Pave Hawks had opened up and we had begun our attack. In a couple of rooms, we had found and captured Sayyaf's wife and rescued a Yazidi slave girl. This is another element of Islamic State I cannot understand. They sate they are religious but happily rape women and children. Forcing young girls into marriage. Tell me what religion allows that? I don't see Islamic State in any way as being religious. It is just an excuse to try to justify what they are doing. They are terrorists pure and simple who have no regard for human life. Many join from countries around the world for the excitement and promises of a good and opulent life at the expense of others.

The operation had been successful. Along with spreadsheet information containing financial data. We also recovered ancient Assyrian artefacts, ancient coins and other priceless artefacts. Along with a wealth of other useful intelligence materials, including cell phones, laptops and documents. As Islamic State also operate heavily in cyber space, any account details, websites and cell numbers aid in tracking individuals and disrupting their operation. Islamic State are the first terrorists to be fighting a war online as well as on the ground. Global recruitment and communications is a key part of Islamic State indoctrination and radicalisation. They have made good use of the so called 'deep web' for communications and money transfer. Even using hard to detect bit coins which are electronic money to finance the purchase of weapons and ammunition including explosives. Such is their use of cyber space, the hacktivists Anonymous have targeted their online operations in retaliation to the Paris and more recent attacks in Brussels. This has led to an online game of cat and mouse between the two groups.

The SAS had not wanted their participation known about to ensure that potential political issues of British boots on the ground in Syria could be avoided. But, the SAS had their cover blown by sources close to the Kurdish government who decided to disclose what role the SAS had played. I am sure the disclosure led to some form of personal gain on their part as well. As the media love, Special Forces stories and the SAS have always been able to steal the headlines ever since the Libyan Embassy siege in London in 1984.

It was said after the raid that more information was obtained from the documents seized in the Sayyaf raid than from "any Special Forces operation in history." This was along with a large stockpile of cash due to the oil operation being largely cashed based. Captured spreadsheets retrieved in the raid showed that Islamic States total natural resource revenues in the six months between September 2014 and February 2015 amounted to $289.5 million. Sayyaf's oil operation in the Deir Ezzour and al-Hasakah provinces in north-eastern Syria contributed to 72 percent of those revenues.

SIX - CLEARENCE

Today, we were going back to check that IS fighters were not trying to re-infiltrate an area just to the north of Qayyarah, Iraq. After a larger Islamic State presence, had been removed often a small number would try to infiltrate and become a nuisance. If needed, we would push them out once more. Islamic State has over the past twelve months began to feel the pressure with personnel losses and a reduction in funding. If Islamic State wanted to stick around, then they would have to throw us out and push back the Iraqi forces.

We moved across a series of fields before stopping short of an intersection with a building on the corner and a few trees. Marc shouted "Over here." I dashed over along with Craig to find several bloody marks in the sandy ground followed by a series of drag marks. The IS fighters had dragged the wounded fighter along with them. Whoever it was, was in a bad way judging from the blood loss. In the current financial squeeze, Islamic State was in. I would have not been surprised if they had been dragged away to have their organs harvested and then sold on the black market before they died. One less IS fighter was not a bad thing no matter how callous that may sound. But the atrocities and complete lack of humanity they had shown to fellow countrymen made you feel that way towards them.

We continued to patrol forwards as the temperature soared into the high 30s. We came across a mosque that had a series of heavy padlocks on all the doors and windows. It was more than likely an Islamic State staging post. We were not permitted to enter unless we had seen enemy activity inside. It would be far better politically and religiously to get the Iraqi Army to check it out. We could call in an air strike but again that could cause political issues locally. Part of fighting a war in another country is to try and not cause issues with the local populous. The British Army call it "winning the hearts and minds" and to be honest it does make sense. It was exactly the same during my two tours in Afghanistan where over time you could get locals to trust you and be almost happy to have soldier's there to stop the Taliban returning and make them feel safe once again.

We continued to patrol for the next five hours moving around the area we had just cleared. Thankfully, we found no sign of Islamic State other than some historical statues that they had purposely torn down. A couple of looted shops and a police station where all the weapons and vehicles had been taken. By now we had just about adapted to the heat and instead of sweating all the time we only sweated when running or wearing our helmets. You still had to hydrate regularly as becoming dehydrated not only slowed you down but could end up making you feel quite ill with headaches, tiredness and even nausea. The other part of patrolling was the concentration and keeping completely aware of your surroundings at all times. Making sure all your arcs were covered. This was very draining in itself without the added extra concern of IEDs, booby traps or mines left as a pleasant surprise for forces re-entering areas once held by Islamic State. Although it was not to the same level as what the Taliban undertook in Afghanistan. The smallest amount of soil out of place or strangely placed boulders could indicate an IED. One of the Russian legacy from their occupation of Afghanistan was the large numbers of mines behind. The Taliban made good use of this free resource and would dig them up. Often stacking two or three mines on top of each other. These would still go off under the weight of a man pretty much blowing them into hundreds of pieces. But their real use was against the various convoys carrying men and equipment around Afghanistan. One big reason is was safer for troops to be moved around in choppers during the war.

In one small deserted village, we climbed onto the roof of a small apartment block three stories high. The stairway was lined with windows which led to an open roof and a good vantage point. In the almost quiet stillness you could almost forget you were in a warzone with danger just around the corner. Parts of Iraq are truly stunning. Something I had not really appreciated until those few moments standing on the apartment roof. I won't say it quite had the same rugged beauty as parts of Afghanistan. Especially the awesome mountainous backdrop on the Afghanistan/Pakistan border. I could see across the village and into the wilderness of the desert. We did not have time to dwell though as you never knew who might be watching us. Standing up there we were sitting ducks for an Islamic State sniper to chalk up another hit.

We made our way back to our vehicles and sped off as dusk fell to the most intense and beautiful display of yellow and orange hues as the sun set. I have never seen a sunset like it before. Iraq like Afghanistan is full of surprises some good and some not so good. But I have grown fond of Iraq during my time here.

SEVEN – PESH SUPPORT

At around 0100 hours, we found our target. We were about half a mile away as we sat and observed the IS fighters. We slowly circled their position taking notes and observing their movements through our night vision goggles. As dawn approached we found a rocky outcrop to hide in and conceal ourselves until nightfall. For the next week, we would be nocturnal operating at night and sleeping during the day. There was just the four of us including myself on this operation – Andy, Craig and Lucas. I was the second longest serving operator in the group. Andy having two more years' service than me. Craig was the baby on his second year of service.

Craig was over six feet tall and sported a thick goatee. He had already provided himself to be up there with the best Delta operators. He was a true twenty first century warrior with an array of technical skills I could only dream of. After joining the 1st Infantry he moved to the 3rd Ranger Battalion. Not long after returning from Afghanistan he found himself going through selection. His physical ability meant he got through the stress phase with ease. It was like he had been born to be an operator. He was already a crack shot when he joined the unit. But, was now even better. He knew the firing ranges, bucket velocity and trajectory of every weapon Delta used. He took some stick though for making the rest of us look bad.

After resting throughout the day, we packed up and as soon as it was dark moved off into the night. We estimated we had a three to four-hour trek to our next reconnaissance point. The final mile to our objective involved crossing an Iraqi motorway. We were deep inside an Islamic State controlled area. They would more than likely have patrols on the motorway. The area we had entered was a hive of activity, with various Islamic Sate patrols going up and down the motorway, randomly stopping vehicles and checking its occupants. If caught, we would be paraded on television before promptly being executed. The propaganda victory for Islamic State would be second to none, even if it caused further world outrage.

The motorway was not going to be an easy task to cross. Using a bridge would make us completely overt and even crossing the motorway we ran the risk of being spotted. Our best bet was to travel alongside the motorway and cross at the darkest point to minimise the chance of being seen.

We ended up trekking several miles to find a safe crossing point. We still had a deep culvert and the motorway itself to navigate across one by one to reduce being seen. Once across motorway they were not that far from the enemy base we needed to gather intelligence on prior to a combined attack with the Kurdish Army. The base was full of activity with trucks containing IS fighters entering and then quite soon afterwards leaving the base. We spent a couple of hours observing the base. Before deciding we needed to get back across the motorway before first light. The raid was to go in and destroy the base and gather as much intelligence as we could. If we could seize a commander's cell phone or laptop we could gather further details on Islamic State members to fulfil the need for an accurate picture to aid in bombing missions and track key Islamic State personnel.

We made it back across the motorway as dawn broke, thankfully being a Sunday morning there was hardly any traffic. Which aided us getting across undetected and back into cover during daylight hours.

After a further forty-eight hours we made it back to base and began the usual planning and briefback prior to assault. The Peshmerga soldiers were used mainly as backup and fire support. Experience had taught us that their haphazard technique of spraying bullets in all directions could lead to vital intelligence being lost. I knew my role in the assault as the sniper was to take out sentries and cover the Delta Team and Peshmerga as they assaulted the base.

The plan of attack was to be dropped in by helicopter about a mile of the mission objective and then use the Osprey as fire support. Delta would be in front with the Kurds at the rear finishing off and then cutting off any fleeing IS fighters. The gates to the base would be breeched with a single Law fired by Craig. I had found a small hill about a quarter of a mile away to set up my snipper rifle and associate kit. I had a spotter with me as well to help with ranges and wind direction.

It was not long before the rest of the team had hit the main entrance road and began to move down it, staying low. Further along, they moved behind a small escarpment that ran alongside the road. The base was surrounded by a wall, behind which there could be a second perimeter fence. After doing a final recce on the objective, it became clear that there were quite a few vehicles, that looked like Toyota Hiluxs, some with weapons, possibly a DSHKs and .50 cal mounted on them along with other IS fighters milling about some carrying RPDs. The Peshmerga's would be on our left flank giving us fire support. The night time sky was darker than normal further aiding us in getting up close to the base unnoticed. We made the assumption that the IS would not think to use night vision goggles, even if they possessed any. Their tactics and the way they fought was almost identical to al-Qaeda having attended the same training camps. Some IS fighters had fought in Afghanistan as well gathering vital knowledge on how U.S. and other forces operated. Craig got his LAW out and fired it. Blowing both the entrance gates off in the process. These massive gates must have gone some twenty feet up in the air before crashing down just missing the IS fighters trying to avoid them.

The initial assault was textbook and IS fighters were initially surprised by the attack. This surprise soon turned to anger and repelling us at all costs. I quickly picked off a couple of IS fighters located on roof tops close to the entrance to the base. The Delta Operators pushed forward, before noticing a pile of sandbags in a corner that looked like an enemy position. This position was empty, so they continued forward another fifty feet. A group of IS fighters all brandishing an AK-47. A couple of them had RPG-7, RPGs. Were currently hiding down the side of an old Iraqi Army truck.

The Delta Operators managed to dive behind a wall just in time. As an American Humvee approached. It was funny as well as a little disconcerting to see an American Humvee driving around complete with a US M240B machine gun mounted on top. The M240B was deadly, firing around 750 -950 7.62 rounds a minute and just over a one mile effective range. Islamic State had managed to capture many American vehicles including M1 Abrahams tanks. Their biggest issue was getting parts to keep them serviceable. The U.S. Governments job was to ensure Islamic State could not get their hands on any parts.

The Peshmerga fire support team got into position. The darkness seemed to have enveloped everything except what was in front of me. As I watched intently through my cross hairs. My mind became focused on the mission, blocking out everything else. Small arms fire had opened up and become quite effective. This was followed by a 12.7mm DSHK. These Russian anti-aircraft guns could churn out 600 rounds per minute. It made a highly effective ground attack weapon that could shred lightly armoured vehicles, tearing through walls and even trees. Tracer rounds were now whizzing across the sky, bringing some limited light to the gloom, before ricocheting or impacting the ground. The Delta Operators were in a full on firefight. Even if some of the IS fighters had no idea which way they should be firing

Small arms fire was now coming from all directions as they drew closer to the main building. It was still wildly inaccurate, but it must not be forgotten that the AK-47 is only accurate to about 50 yards, it is much better at putting plenty of rounds down with good short range stopping power. Some IS fighters are very good at what they do; however, the majority are poor shots having only received very basic training. It is their tenacity and will to fight to the death that makes them such a danger. At times like the Taliban, I am positive they have been high on drugs and continued to advance even with quite serious injuries.

One of the guys managed to get a couple of rounds into a DShK gunner. The rounds hit the gunner side on, pushing him slightly side wards before he slumped forward over the DShK, and for an instant it fell silent. But a split second later a second fighter had climbed onto the weapon, and the DShKs gaping muzzle began spitting fire in our direction once more.

Once inside the main building, an assault team had been allocated a floor. My job then switched to preventing anyone else entering the building almost acting as flank protection. A fierce firefight raged on inside the building as Delta operators overwhelmed and killed everyone inside the building. Picking up any worthwhile intelligence as they went. Bodies were checked for cell phones and anything else of use. We had a small window of time as Islamic State reinforcements would have been alerted the moment we began our assault. Some reinforcements had begun to arrive as we made our escape.

It was going to be a slow fighting retreat as thousands of rounds buzzed all round us as more IS fighters seem to pop up, almost as if they had been buried in the ground and we were in the midst of some form of zombie apocalypse. The Peshmerga continued to offer fire support, but our own fire support needed to pull back as well, with us giving them covering fire, as they made a hasty retreat to our evacuation point. I managed to take out a couple of IS fighters as we made our fighting retreat. Before they gave up and let us flee into the night, possibly hoping another patrol my find us and finish us off. The mission was considered a success. We had gathered up highly useful intelligence that would be useful for planning and coordination of further attacks. It would also aid us in the training of Peshmerga, giving them valuable insight and intelligence into Islamic State to aid in planning further operations and raids. The base was then obliterated by a couple of bombs from RAF Typhoon jets so it could not be re-occupied by them.

EIGHT - PATRIOT

We continued to work with the Iraqi Army our missions typically would take us ahead of their main advance scouting for positions and enemy strongholds. Often to get to these strongholds we had to fight or go around 'friction points.' We knew Islamic State had a few positions in the area of Tikrit. Whilst Islamic State had a stronghold in and around Mosul and towards Baiji they still only really had thin strips of land. The areas they operated in however was much larger, simply due to the size of Iraq. Between 2014 and 2016 Islamic State has lost around 40% of the populated territory it once had in Iraq. Air strikes alone have killed an estimated 25,000 IS fighters in Syria and Iraq. 600 hundred of those in the first three months of 2016. This has cut Islamic States strength in half; but it is not just the number of fighters which have been cut but also its finance stream from selling oil on the black market. At its peak Islamic State was estimated to be earning $1.4 million a day from selling oil alone. With repeated airstrikes on oilfields this funding stream has been reduced by a third. Such is the financial impact that IS fighters had their salaries cut in half to $200 to $700 a day depending on rank. It is believed that Islamic State only has around 30,000 fighters. They are even removing organs from injured IS fighters to sell on the black market to help raise funds. The large profits Islamic State made from oil was the main reason it was decided to target Islamic States oil infrastructure with air strikes. By reducing Islamic States ability to produce oil and profitability has in reduced income. Even after 30 percent of the oil infrastructure had been destroyed Islamic State was still making $1 million a day from the sale of crude oil. Islamic State maintains its oil production by offering handsome salaries to skilled oil workers. These workers earn at least three times the average Syrian salary of $50 per month for an accountant. This goes up to eight times the average salary per month for a drilling technician.

Islamic State at one point was able to easily get new recruits from around the world not just for oil production but the foot soldiers required to attack and hold territory. The recruits were able to pour into Iraq and Syria using a wide-open stretch of rugged border. This stretch became known as the 'Gateway to Jihad'. An example of one border crossing not far from Reyhanli, Turkey is just a dry, dusty track that snakes its way up to and then across the border from Turkey into Syria. It is one of the ancient smuggling routes crisscrossing over the hills to Syria, the border is marked by nothing more than the odd scraps of barbed wire. The path leads down to the Orontes River, which meanders through the valley of olive plantations, and on the other side is Syria. This where an alarmingly easy route to enter Syria. Border guards would even turn a blind eye for as little as $10. It was estimated that at its peak around 20 foreign recruits were travelling through it each day on this poorly policed border area, of mountain passes and plains without confronting security. Once in eastern Turkey, recruits hook up with Islamic State handlers and embark on spending sprees in local army equipment shops. They could buy hunting knives, sniper rifle sights, binoculars and desert camouflage fatigues. There is an example of one IS fighter who walked into a shop waving $50,000 in bundles of cash as he bought a thousand 'magazine vests' for carrying spare AK-47 rifle ammunition clips. Turkey was initially reluctant to stop anyone from crossing. Allowing weapons and supplies destined for recognised Syrian opposition groups to cross. Although, this flow of new recruits has been reduced dramatically since Turkey tightened its border security succumbing to European and U.S. pressure. It has helped control the number of new recruits replenishing those that have been lost. A steady ramping up of military operations in Iraq will only see their numbers drop further. More boots on the ground are to be sent along with Apache helicopters, which more than proved there worth in Afghanistan and both Iraq wars. On Monday 21 April 2016, B-52 bombers were used for the first time to carry out a bombing mission on Islamic State weapons storage facility near the town Qayyarah, Iraq. The B-52s had not long arrived at Al Udeid Air Base in Qatar before being deployed replacing B-1B Lancer bombers as the primary bomber in Syria and Iraq. The B-52 can carry a mighty payload and has proven its destructive power with its ability to destroy vast swaths of rain forest during the Vietnam War.

The prize for Islamic State is still Baghdad with IS units being sent in to wreak havoc. Although the number has dwindled over the past twelve months. More often than not their attack has been foiled and they have been taken out before their assault could begin with an airstrike. Islamic State has not been able to mount a successful offensive operation since Ramadi and Palmyra in May 2015. Moreover, whenever it has tried the attack has been smashed quickly and efficiently, typically suffering 60 percent or higher casualties than is was previously. Islamic State in its current state is like a boxer in the final rounds of a fight who won't go on for much long before they are knocked out. Although, they will get back up and continue to be a problem for some time to come. Training harder and trying again to take a swing at various countries. With more terrorist attacks on individual nations in an attempt to bring governments to accept their demands.

However, even if pushed out of Syria and Iraq they will move to a new area. They will continue to indoctrinate and radicalise young minds around the world. They will continue to mount terrorist attacks such as the ones in Paris and Brussels. All the world can do is be vigilant and try to stamp out the radicalisation in the first place. Religious communities have their part to play in making sure concerns over individuals are passed onto the authorities. Those at danger of being radicalised are supported by their community and not given a reason to be radicalised in the first place.

We darted around Iraq as a platoon of sixteen men to take on any stronger resistance we came across. On one occasion, we were coming towards an IS base when a patrol outside the perimeter spotted us. The firefight started off as the odd pot shot but quickly ratcheted up as IS fighters seemed to come pouring in from all directions. This was one hell of a firefight with rounds flying around in all directions. I stared to take down IS fighter after IS fighter with my Colt Model 727 or CAR 15 assault rifle. It was like playing a video game with the enemy respawning. We called in for air support, but that was going to be delayed. The firefight lasted for a couple of hours, with the fire seeming to die down for a while before stoking up again. In most firefights, it would last for maybe a few minutes to maybe an hour depending on the numbers of fighters we were engaging. This firefight just seemed to go on and on. They were steadily advancing on our position and if air support did make it to us we would get caught in the blast. We had no choice but to make a fighting retreat, just as we thought, "shit, we are going to die if don't escape" a pair of F-18s came rolling in and dropped a couple of bombs right in the middle of the IS fighters. The explosion ripped through them. I saw arms, leg and other body parts flying off in all directions as a giant yellow and orange plume stretched out into the sky. The amount of dust caused by the explosion virtually blinded us. As the dust settled other than the odd bit of sporadic fire, air support had saved our butts big time.

We used the explosion to make good our escape and returned back to base to a gleeful head shed. Not because we had won, but because we had made it all back alive and he did not want to lose any one else. When soldier's start to die especially lots of them, public opinion starts to change. You only have to look at Vietnam and to a much lesser extent Afghanistan. The big reason there are not more U.S. boots on the ground is down to politics more than anything else.

I am not embarrassed to say, I am a patriot through and through and get stuck in with whatever the politicians tell me to do via my commanders. I love my country and opportunities it has given me. The National Anthem still causes my stomach to knot each time I hear it. Out here in Iraq the words "land of the free" and "home of the brave" have a poignant meaning. That is what we fight for – to try to give countries in need the chance to have what we have in America. The freedom to speak out, the freedom to be heard, the freedom to be who we want to be. I am sure some individuals and human rights type people may disagree, but that is what the American constitution is built on. You only have to see how Islamic State treat its local populous to realize how much freedom we have as a U.S. citizen.

NINE – CLOSE CALL

I stood up through the hatch of an Iraqi Humvee observing a small group of buildings when an RPG whizzed to my right. Everyone opened up including me on the .50 cal. The IS fighters responded with a few burst of fire but we kept the pressure on them with a large volume of fire. RPGs are not nice - especially when they burst as they shower the impact area with shrapnel. RPGs continued to be fire at us one after another. Whenever we saw the dust that flew up from where they were launched, we concentrated our fire on those locations.

Marc spotted a window from which some of the RPGs were being fired from. That soon had a large number of rounds being pumped through the window. Then an RPG flew past just a couple of yards above my head. I dropped down into the Humvee just as it hit the ground and caused the vehicle to shudder from the blast wave. Craig let off a LAW and scored a direct hit. The rate of enemy fire suddenly dropped dramatically. Small arms fire was still flying around us along with the odd RPG. I then spotted a building where enemy fire was coming from. I shouted to the rest of the team "Over there, large two storeys building with four windows." I switched to my MK-14 and whilst the guys got fire onto the positon. I lined my scope up ready to take a shot. I quickly set up for wind speed and distance. Just as I was about to fire, a blinding flash filled my scope as another RPG left the window. I could barely make out the outline of the figure holding the RPG but let off three rounds in quick succession. It was too dark inside the building to see if I had hit him or not. All I knew, was that no more RPGs were fired from that window. The rest of the team moved forward to clear the buildings whilst I acted as overwatch from my Humvee. Rifle at the ready to take out any IS fighters who posed a threat or were trying to flee. The odd IS fighter was dropped by the guys as they entered one building. However, other than a couple of IS fighters found and killed inside. The threat had been neutralized and eight IS fighters lay dead across two buildings. Their bodies were searched for intelligence before we re-grouped, mounted up and headed towards the next village. In many ways, the IS fighters did fight in a very similar way as the Taliban had in Afghanistan and much of what we learnt about the enemy there has been transferable. IS fighters like the Taliban wear no insignia so the usual sniper tactic of taking out a higher ranking officer is much harder unless you know exactly who they are.

The Taliban for instance did not like to stay still and shoot. They would much rather use flanking manoeuvres and engaged us with tactics that needed to be picked up early on. They knew we could bring down heavier firepower than they had. A quick ambush or setting numerous IEDs could yield better results for them. An IED was a good way to slow a convoy down then ambush it and kill as many American or coalition forces as they could. Islamic State have not used quite the same tactics, but are very similar some having been through the same training camps. The Taliban like Islamic State found using mopeds or motorbikes a good way of getting about as was a harder target to locate and hit. On one occasion in Afghanistan, I remember nearing a small village a few miles away from Jalalabad going in for a typical 'snatch' raid on a Taliban commander. As we got close to the village we started to watch a local teenager on a moped who kept driving at speed across the front of us at a range of about 400 yards to the front of us. As soon as he came to a standstill I got my scope out to see if I could see what weapons if any he was carrying. Using a technique called 'baseline' a technique that has come from Israel. That states you look out for something that looks different to what you would expect to see. What you would normally expect to see is called the baseline. He stood out as he was the only local remaining in the area while the remainder of the locals were all heading away as quickly as possible.

We knew from experience he must be a Taliban spotter. The British, especially the SAS were very aware of this having come across it before in Northern Ireland. Here these spies were given the nickname 'dickers' and the British Army used the same term in Afghanistan for Taliban spies. 'Dickers' was the name given to spies back in Northern Ireland during the time of the Irish Republican Army. The spies were usually unassuming civilians who would relay messages of the positions of British forces. The same happened in Afghanistan; these 'dickers' could be anything from children to tribal elders. They would use cell phones, smoke, mirrors or even kites, which the Taliban had once banned, to report back the movement and strength of coalition forces. They got paid for any information they passed on.

Craig decided the best bet would be to give him a warning shot. As the moped approached us once again near to a junction. Craig fired a round from his M4. The round whizzed past in front of the moped. The shock of the round caused the lad on it to nearly drop his moped on the floor catching it just in time. With that he got his moped upright jumped back on it and sped off into the distance, probably having had the fright of his life.

We finally reached the village and dismounted. I made my way to the roof of the tallest building to act as overwatch. The rest of the team made their way through meandering buildings. The village was eerily quiet. Although not that unusual as the occupants of villagers such as these would flee from the advancing Islamic State. Knowing all too well what they would do to the occupants especially the women and girls. The team continued to patrol through looking into doorways, but the whole village seemed completely deserted.

All of a sudden, a shot rang out and everyone took cover by getting down low huddling into a couple of doorways. I swung my scope round to where the noise of the shot had come from and we all waited for further shots to come. There was obviously someone about and we had no idea if it was friend or foe. After a few minutes, had passed and nothing further the guys continued to push forward only a little more cautiously now. As they turned a corner they were spotted by some malnourished dogs. All four of them were skin and bone with matted fur and looked in a pitiful state. They stood there snarling and growling a couple were foaming at the mouth. The team decided just to ignore them and carried on. Had one decided to attack then it would have had to have been shot. The team finally made it to the far edge of the village and saw no one.

As they were about to turn around had head back a burst of gunfire flew over their head and they dropped to the ground rolling towards the side of the building to get into better cover. I had seen the muzzle flash from a small hill on the far side of the village. I waited for the IS fighter to pop back up so I could get a round into his head. I waited and waited but nothing happened. The rest of the team decided to crawl back down the way they had come from. I knew there had to be more IS fighters out there.

Just then my question was answered when an RPG came flying from over the hill and hit the area the Delta guys had just vacated. I still could not see anything and the rest of the team got some fire down as they retreated backwards. They decided to get themselves into a compound and onto the roof for a better vantage point. Once on the roof they began to fire off short bursts of fire at the hill. Hoping the IS fighter or fighters may pop out so I could get a shot off. Once again nothing happened and we waited for the next burst of fire or RPG.

The volley of fire finally came from our right flanks. The IS fighters had managed to move around unnoticed and get another burst of fire off at the rest of the team on the compound roof. The team opened up on the IS fighters position. Finally, I spotted a fighter in a group of trees to my far right. It seemed as if they were trying to circle us and then attack from the rear flank.

My shot found its target hitting the fighter on the top of his head and blowing his head apart. We had no idea of strength, but that at least was one fighter out of the picture. It was a case of sitting, watching and waiting for someone to appear with another volley of fire.

We waited and waited and nothing happened. Rather than wait for a much larger Islamic State force to appear we decided the best idea was to get out of the village and move back into the desert.

Even as we mounted up there was nothing to be heard. Had we really been pinned down by a lone IS fighter or was the rest of the force waiting to ambush us? That is an answer we will never know. We mounted up and headed off back into the desert without hearing a further shot or seeing anyone else. The more IS fighters we could capture or kill would reduce their strength. If we could reduce their strength faster than they could recruit, we could turn the course of the war on Islamic State much quicker.

During the second Gulf War JSOC's Delta-led campaign in Iraq was on a scale never previously accomplished by a relatively small group of highly trained forces. It was estimated afterwards that something in the region of 3000 insurgents had been killed along with another 9000 captured. Such was the number of insurgents killed or removed from the streets the level of violence in Iraq dropped dramatically. This help both the coalition and Iraqi partners, the Anbar Awakening, which Sunni communities along turn against al-Qaeda and the ceasefire agreement with Moqtada al-Sadr's Shi'a militia, the Mahdi Army reclaim back the streets of Iraq. Even factoring that in JSOC's amazing industrial counterterrorism campaign turned the tide. Delta effectively broke al-Qaeda in Iraq by killing and capturing its members faster than replacements could be recruited.

TEN - DRONES

The Osprey lifted off into the night sky. In the rear, it carried a M1161 Growler Light Strike Vehicle (LSV). These compact and lightweight (two tonne) vehicles have minimal ballistic or blast protection. They are powered by a 2.8 litre four-cylinder diesel with 132bhp with a top speed of 85 mph on a road. They are designed to be able to go off-road to avoid mines and IEDs. They are a step up from the DPVs we have also used. I was already sitting in the driver's seat of the Growler as we came into land. The ramp dropped and I hit the Gas speeding off into the night. I hit a soft patch and the Growler veered to the right, I had to put in opposite lock to carry on going forward. The other two Growlers started to check in over the radio and we regrouped about a mile away from the landing zone. We had an area of operations to again go in and perform recognisance. Some of this was to be done by eyeball and some of it was to be undertaken by drones in the form of the PD-100 Black Hornet. The PD-100 UAV itself is 10 × 2.5 cm and weighs 16g. It can fly for around 20 minutes with a classified range. It takes about 20 minutes to learn ow to fly it. The Brits first used them in Afghanistan. By 2013 they had 324 in service. U.S. Forces started testing them in March 2015. We are now testing an upgraded version of the PD-100 to see how we get on. Marines Special Operations have also been testing the PD-100. It is a good piece of kit even if the actual helicopter looks a bit like a toy. You control the UAV with a joystick with several buttons and what is best described as a tablet which gives a live feed of what the UAV is seeing. Control of the drone is semi-automatic via movement buttons. GPS is used to locate enemy positions or items of interest; these can then be used for airstrikes or to plan how an attack will be undertaken. It is fitted with three cameras and the latest Black Hornet has both long-wave infrared and day video sensors that can transmit video streams or high-resolution still images via a digital data-link with a 1-mile range.

As British Army Major Adam Foden said:

"Black Hornet is a game-changing piece of kit. Previously we would have sent soldiers forward to see if there were any enemy fighters hiding inside a set of

buildings. Now we are deploying Black Hornet to look inside compounds and to clear a route through enemy-held spaces. It has worked very well and the pictures it delivers back to the monitor are really clear. And Black Hornet is so small and quiet that the locals can't see or hear it.

We continued our drive into the desert looking for a suitable place to hide before dawn broke. We chose and area away from where Islamic State were known to be operating. Although that would not mean we could not be detected by a patrol. Although it was rare for them to venture so deep into the desert. They much preferred to stay close to their territory and repel attacks from ourselves or Iraqi forces.

Islamic State has been described as one of the richest militant groups in the world. In June 2014, when the group took over the city of Mosul, Islamic State reportedly plundered a government vault at the Mosul Central Bank, taking millions in state money (high estimates place the total amount the group looted as $ 1.5 billion). It has seized oil fields in Syria and Iraq and is allegedly making significant money selling Syrian and Iraqi crude on the black market; most recently, France has accused the Syrian regime of Bashar Assad of purchasing its own oil from Islamic State. Additionally, it has been reported that Islamic State makes millions through kidnapping and ransoms, involvement in the smuggling and underground trade of stolen Iraqi antiquities, and extortion in the areas it has conquered.

Islamic State have become masters of using social media as a weapon. In previous times, advancing armies smoothed their path with bombardments or missiles before launching an attack. Islamic State instead made use of social media to achieve the same result with tweets and a movie. This social media propaganda worked in Mosul where Iraqi soldiers fled their posts. It was thought that thirty-thousand Iraqi troops fled in terror from 800 IS fighters. They feared they would face a gruesome fate if they were captured by IS fighters in uniform.

Islamic State has made use of an app called the Dawn of Glad Tidings. This app has allowed Islamic State to use their accounts to send out centrally written updates. Released simultaneously, the messages swamp social media, giving Islamic State a far larger online reach than their own accounts would otherwise allow. The Dawn app pumps out news of the terror group's advances, gory images, or frightening videos like Swords IV – creating the impression of an uncontrollable and unstoppable force. All of this propaganda is designed to put fear into their enemies at the same time aiding in moral of IS fighters.

The next day we were given orders via our Satcom to clear a building a few miles away to our south. A local commander was doing his 'rounds.' Our job was to take him out. We decided to go in on foot for the last mile concealing our rides behind a large sand dune. We had 'glassed' the target to look for suitable entrance points and further intelligence. A Predator drone was going to aid us as our eye in the sky, courtesy of the CIA.

The MQ-1 Predator was originally conceived in the early 1990s for aerial reconnaissance and forward observation roles. It carries a variety of cameras and other sensors. It is also able to carry and fire two AGM-114 Hellfire missiles or other munitions. The war against Islamic State has seen their retirement pushed from 2015 to 2018.

We would use the fundamental Delta principle of "surprise, speed and violence of action." This principle states that if you lose one element you increase on the next. An example would be to lose surprise and therefore increase the pace. At the breach or entry point if it was obvious that the enemy knew we were coming. We would escalate to an even more violent explosive entry.

It does not matter how Delta reaches the objective, the expression "slow is smooth, smooth is fast" is the doctrine applied when conducting close quarter combat or CBQ. If you watch Delta operators "free flow" CBQ on targets without having a floor plan is a sight to behold. It may not look sequenced but the Delta operators sweep through a building almost effortlessly. This is where our extensive amount of time in the' killing house' pays off with each operator knowing instinctively how to flow as a team. This includes being able to place two shots into an eye socket at 50 feet – known as the "double tap." To those being assaulted they often only see dark figures behind the flash form the flash bangs before meeting their maker. It is perhaps Delta's signature skill that is unmatched by any other special force.

It only took a matter of minutes to get the PD-100 UAV ready to go before I held it up and launched it from my hand, flying towards a potential Islamic State position, the idea was to fly in and observe the area around, looking at strength and enemy armour which Islamic State had at his location. We also wanted to get eyes on the main target and look for a suitable assault point. Marc flew the PD-100 in and it quickly found a couple of BMPs which Marc clicked on the screen to get their GPS co-ordinates which could be used for a bombing run/ The PD-100 UAV quickly made it over the area to be recce'd, before starting a further sweep and picking up twenty Islamic State fighters and a single T-72. It looked un-operational but its co-ordinates were also taken. It was time to bring the PD-100 in and pass on our intelligence and co-ordinates. These were quickly passed onto a pair of RAF GR4 Tornado jets which had been diverted from another fire support mission. As the Tornados made their way in. A Predator drone loitering in the area would be brought in to assess the damage and follow our assault.

With the enemy armor destroyed it was our turn to go in and take the local commander out. It would have been great f I could have just taken him out with a sniper round. But, Islamic State had realized that they needed to better protect key figures from potential sniper fire. After successful operations by the SAS and other special forces at taking out key personnel at long range. We kept low and moved at speed towards our objective. It was a case of simply following the acrid black smoke emanating from the various vehicles that had been obliterated by a handful of bombs. We faced no resistance as we made it inside the compound. As soon as we stepped inside small arms fire opened up sending chunks of the compound walk flying off in all directions. One small chunk bouncing off my lightweight Kevlar helmet.

Instinctively we hunted for a target and Craig quickly did a double tap before we pushed forward sliding along the walls and clearing each room. We found no further resistance and other than a couple of females who were secured and later turned out to be Kurdish sex slaves. There was no one else in the building. Cell phones and any other intelligence was secured. Before we made our way back out and into the relative safety of the desert.

It would later turn out the IS commander had been burnt to a crisp in the BMP he had decided to hide in to escape sniper fire. He had been tipped off that an attack was imminent but had not counted on bombs from above! Islamic State has become all too aware of being spotted by drones and changed its tactics accordingly. However, this has only had limited success. Jihadi John being one who was finally neutralized by a drone attack as he stepped into his car on November 12, 2015. With not much left of 'Jihadi John' other than an 'oily stain on the ground.'

Jihadi John was behind the killing of American journalist James Foley along with others. His real name was Mohammed Emwazi was originally from Kuwait and moved to England in 1994 when he was six. Mohammed was a member of a secret Osama Bin Laden sleeper cell based in Britain called 'The London Boys', which planned to carry out atrocities in the West. He was involved with a violent street gang who targeted the wealthy residents of Belgravia, Central London with stun guns. He was being tracked by the British Mi5 as a known terrorist. Mohammed saw himself as the victim and on the verge of suicide due to the intrusion by the British security services. Mohammed believed himself to be a victim. He knew Mi5 were closing in on him. He decided to flee England and join Islamic State. His travelling companion Ibrahim Magag said in an ISIS magazine. *"In the end, we decided to travel hidden in a lorry – controls are much stricter entering the UK than they there leaving."*

The two of them got to France in the back of a lorry, carrying £30,000 with them when they left England. From France, they then travelled on to Belgium where they shaved off their hair and beards. They also bought new clothes to disguise their identities. They were quite easily able to book flights to Albania, confident that British intelligence would not have shared their details with the Belgian authorities. Despite looking at their passports, the Belgian authorities did not stop them and they could board the flights and make their way to Greece. From there, an ISIS fixer helped them get a boat across to Turkey and get across the border into Syria so they could join Islamic State. Emwazi would soon gain notoriety as 'Jihadi John' for orchestrating at least six hostage murders in Syria along with James Foley.

We were told to get ourselves back to base. Much to our annoyance, but command could still be jittery at times at to reduce the potential for American losses. They would much rather use bombs or even Iraqi security forces. Dead American soldiers was not good politically especially after Afghanistan.

ELEVEN - NUTJOBS

Barely an hour had passed from our briefing and we were in a Pave Hawk about to cross the border into Syria. It was a warm night so we had the doors open and our feet tucked in as we peered into the inky black night. We were flying over the featureless desert, before banking hard and turning to the east. I caught the outline of several palm trees. Our birds were now hugging the ground as we got in close to avoid radar detection. Trees and vegetation would not only hide us from view but also help screen the noise from the rotors and twin turbine engines. I made a mental note of the terrain as we flew over it, using the map of the area in my head to get a rough idea of our position. Should we get shot down it would help enormously with our subsequent escape and evasion.

This operation had led to a quick brief back and kit check. The whole mission was based on local intelligence and an 'eye in the sky.' We only had an approximation of the numbers of IS fighters at the objective which was believed to be fifteen. This included an Islamic State intelligence officer which was our objective. The CIA had gathered the intelligence and then used one of their Predator drones to verify it. A drone strike was normally used but the potential for intelligence especially cell phone intelligence was felt that special forces could both take out the target and gather any useful intelligence.

We were now a couple of minutes out and time to do a final weapons and kit check. Our birds began to slow down and we prepared to jump off the minute the Pave Hawks wheels touched the ground. The moment we hit the ground we leapt out and quickly made for our objective. It was a small compound in the middle of nowhere. A perfect Islamic State hideout. It had sentries positioned on the roof as well as a roving guard walking round the perimeter.

We made use of some long grass and thick vegetation for cover. As we got close we could hear voices in some of the nearby compounds. I notice that the lights inside were flickering,

We were sure that there would be people looking out or on the roof, but through our NVGs we could not see anyone positioned up there.

Undertaking an early morning raid helped, as many fighters would be asleep and reduced potential contact, even though once we were in and shooting, the rest of the fighters would soon be woken up by the commotion.

We had an RC-135 circling above along with a predator drone keeping a watchful eye and collecting a live video feed of the operation. This would be used by our commanders and CIA as well as in our 'hot wash' debrief later. An eye in the sky meant we had extra eyes who not only could see the attack from above but could pass on vital real time intelligence as we commenced our attack. This could be the locations of IS fighters or incoming reinforcements. It also meant anyone who tried to make a hasty retreat could be quickly tracked and eliminated if necessary.

I looked at my watch and it was 0215 hours and ready to launch our assault. We would need a quick breach and quick elimination of any IS fighters we found. The greater the surprise and speed the less chance they would have to offer and form of co-ordinated response.

Walking along huddled down as low as we could get, I caught sight of a IS fighter through the green hues of my NVGs. I could also pick out the bright white glow of a light above the main entrance to the compound. A AC-130U Spooky II with its General Dynamics 25mm GAU-12/U Equalizer Gatling cannon, 40 mm L/60 Bofors cannon and 105 mm M102 howitzer. Would act as fire support and used to take out any fleeing IS fighters. This meant we did not have to worry about putting a cut off in place.

The plan was for a simultaneous frontal assault on several of the buildings that made up the compound. The idea was to go in and take out anything we found moving, if we could take the intelligence officer alive, we would. It was highly unlikely he would give us any intelligence unless we could 'persuade' him that working for us was a better option. But as these Islamic State nutjobs believed in martyrdom. Which is basically suffering or dying for your beliefs. While it might not sound pleasant, to those in Islamic State it's a great honor. The root of martyrdom is the Greek word martur, which means "witness.

Back at base on giant monitors. The white shapes that represented us could be seen moving up towards the compound. We were no fifty feet from our objective and had luckily still not been spotted.

I glanced over my shoulder to see that everyone was formed up ready to. I used hand signals to direct the operators to the three entry points on the compound.

I was attacking the main target along with Marc and we stacked up at the door waiting to burst in. All three entry points would be breached simultaneously. In total, we had eight operators. Two stacked up at each of the entry points and a further two acting as cover.

One by one we got on the radio and said, "In position." Finally, after a minute, I gave the order to begin the assault.

Marc reached out and carefully tried the door handle. No point kicking the door down if the door was unlocked. By chance it was unlocked as Marc gently pushed it open his NVGs probing the room half expecting an IS fighter to open up on us the moment we put a foot inside. I could feel sweat trickling down my face, as even though it was the early hours, it was still very warm. There was nobody in there. There could be someone hiding under the floorboards, but we doubted this and moved onto the next building to support the other two teams.

The remainder of the team had swiftly gone through the building double tapping anything that moved or was asleep in a bed. Thankfully, there was no women or children in this compound. That always complicated matters and tied up operators whilst they were dealt with and taken out of harm's way.

I spotted the nose of a battered Toyota Hilux poking around the corner of one building. Its red paint had faded in places. It had seen plenty of action judging from the number of dents and scrapes on the front fender and down the sides. This same Toyota had been seen conveying our target around the local area. We knew we were in the right place, we just had to locate him. Just as I was about to check the Toyota out I heard the sound of an AK-47 opening up just to my right from a roof top. Marc spun round and as the expert marksman that he is fired off a couple of rounds. These hit the IS fighter in the chest and the face. Partially blowing his face off in the process. The IS fighters hail of fire had missed both of us completely. Either he was a lousy shot or could not actually see us in the dark.

The AK-47 ringing out alerted the rest of the IS fighters that they must be under attack and our element of surprise was gone. We needed to ensure our target did not flee and quickly picked up the pace to get the area secured. I ran with Marc into the building we be believed the IS intelligence officer was hiding.

On entering I found another IS fighter inside his weapon spat out a hail of bullets. I opened up firing down the main corridor of the building. Marc did not realise until later a single round had hit his body armour and saved his life. The house had all its lights on, so our NVGs were rendered useless. We quickly continued room by room clearance being all too aware of potential booby traps. There were several rooms off the main corridor and each one would need to be searched and cleared. With our presence now know we flung in stun grenades into a couple of the rooms.

The first flash bang went off with the usual flash and crackle. We moved on to the next room, Marc threw the flash bang in and went in first, he let off several rounds taking out two IS fighters who had only just awoke, probably from the noise of the first flash bang. The IS fighters AK-47s lay on the floor next to their beds. They were promptly killed before they had a chance to grab them and use them on us.

We pushed up the main corridor before rounding the door to the last room, with my weapon levelled as I went in. I saw a man in his early thirties with a long brown beard wearing a black dish-dash. He had more hair on his chin than his head. His eyes were filled with hatred and rage. He had the look of someone who felt we were beneath him and how dare us enter his living quarters.

I had no idea what he would do next and saw he was holding an automatic pistol. Without thinking I did a double tap to the head watching blood splatter onto the creamy brown wall behind him. Before he dropped to the floor. Marc quickly searched him, seizing two cell phones, whilst I did a search of the room picking up any papers or personal affects that could be of interest to us. That was the last room and final building out of the three to be cleared. Nine IS fighters lay dead within the compound and another two had been taken out by the Spooky flying above as they tried to escape.

With no time to waste we re-grouped checked for injuries and quickly made our way back to the pick-up point with our Pave Hawks waiting to whisk us away back into Iraq and relative safety of our base. It was an uneventful trip back to base. That is the best sort of journey. With no injuries, the target eliminated and a useful amount of intelligence gathered it was a successful op. Now it was time for the usual debrief followed by chow.

TWELVE - BIRD

Islamic State has been operating independently of other jihadist groups in Syria such as the al-Nusra Front, the official al-Qaeda affiliate in the country, and has had a tense relationship with other rebels. They have had a limited amount of military success with the capture of Raqqa in 2014. Baghdadi the leader of Islamic State sought to merge with al-Nusra, which went on to reject the deal, and the two groups have operated separately since. Zawahiri an al-Qaeda chief has urged ISIS to focus on Iraq and leave Syria to al-Nusra, but Baghdadi and his fighters openly defied Zawahiri. Hostility to Islamic State has grown steadily in Syria as Islamic State regularly attacked fellow rebels and abused civilian supporters of the Syrian opposition. The Russian offensive in Syria has targeted in the main Islamic State. But, has also targeted some of the rebel forces as well in order to aid government forces regaining control of the country since the start of the uprising in spring 2011.

We crossed into of Syria at the tail end of a sandstorm, just as the first rays of dawn light broke through. The ground below was a mixture sand dunes and tall rocky outcrops. We were all on a high state of alert as we entered hostile territory. It was not long before we could hear gunfire. The shots initially sounded scattered but as we got closer the fire became more and more intense. Tracer fire along with rounds of various calibre began to whip round us.

Then a round finally found its mark and hit a fire extinguisher setting it off and filling the cockpit with white smoke. Having a round actually finding its mark heightened our situational awareness. Another round whizzed through the open doors just missing all of us. The ground fire seemed to intensify as I saw a couple of RPGs head our way before harmlessly detonating below us. The door gunner was swivelling around firing at targets on the ground below as another round punched through the outer skin and cut through a wiring loom. The cockpit lit up like a Christmas tree as numerous warning lights flashed up on the console. Further tracer rounds whizzed above and below us lighting up the night's sky. The navigator then took a small flesh wound as a round nicked his left leg. Things were starting to turn serious. Our bird did not seem to want to fly the same as the pilots wrestled to maintain control. We had no choice but to turn around and head for home. The operation for us was cancelled and handed over to a drone strike instead.

Another round then hit the plexiglass on the door and showered us in a shower of hot plastic. The door gunner continued to hammer out rounds at what was believed to be IS fighters below, but it could have been rebel forces who thought we were government forces. Our job was simply to survive and outrun this firestorm that we had found ourselves in.

Another blast from an RPG detonating a bit too close for comfort rocked the bird violently from side to side. Another round pierced the outer skin and hit a hydraulic line, thankfully being deflected instead of doing any damage. The Pave Hawk like the Black Hawk it is based on has three hydraulic pumps and associated systems along with a self-sealing valves to reduce leaks. Hydraulic fluid is to a helicopter what blood is to us. A bullet then ripped through the bottom of the chopper before exiting out of the open side door. I hung out of the side door of the bird again to check on the other helicopter. It seemed to us that because we were flying in front of the other bird, we were taking most of the fire. Rounds had been fired at the other bird but not one of them had actually hit it. I turned back to hang outside again to try to see if we were finally starting to outrun this firestorm. It did seem that the number of rounds being fired had dramatically reduced.

These Pave Hawks are some damn tough birds; this was the most amount of fire I had received in a chopper even after Afghanistan. Where we had taken the odd round but nothing like this. The whole ordeal had lasted only a few minutes but it seemed much longer than that. In the air you cannot take cover behind a building you rely on speed or altitude to get away as quickly as possible. As in the air there is nothing for you to hide behind and can only fly through or over a threat. When you can see tracer rounds coming at you, you know that for every one tracer round there is at least another four rounds you cannot see. We continued our flight back to base warning lights still flashing away in the cockpit but our bird was still flying. Finally, we were back at base as we hit the tarmac hard and bounced to a stop.

We quickly got off and as the rotors wound down helped get the co-pilot out and off for medical attention. We then inspected our wounded bird. It was as we were walking around Craig noticed I had been hit in the shoulder. As the webbing on my body armour had been partially torn. It was one hell of a lucky shot and a lucky escape for me. You could see several holes all over the pave hawk, the odd one was weeping fluid but nothing serious. The plexiglass on one of the side doors had shattered and there was at least three holes in the nose of the chopper. This is where the badass 160th pilots earn their pay, keeping so cool and collected under enemy fire even whilst being wounded themselves.

Craig had a sad, hang-dog look on his face. I decided I'd lighten up his attitude. "Hey, man, how's it going, you're not hurt, are you?" The shock from what had just happened had obviously hit him. I slapped him on his back and he replied, "I'm okay, I guess."

After watching the news and seeing the atrocities in Brussels changed Craig's shock to anger as yet again Islamic State had targeted innocent victims with suicide bombs. Continuing their so called 'Jihad' in the most violent way possible.

The term Jihad translates from Arabic as struggle. It is used to denote a religious duty of
Muslims. A person engaged in jihad is called a mujahid; the plural is mujahedeen. This term was used for the multi-national insurgent groups in Afghanistan fighting against the Soviet's occupation of Afghanistan from 1979 to the decision by the Soviets withdraw in 1989. The word jihad appears frequently in the Quran the religious text of Islam. The term Jihad within the Quran is often in the idiomatic expression "striving in the way of God." In Shia Islam Jihad is one of the ten Practices of the Religion. However, Jihad is often translated into "holy war." If military jihad is required to protect the Muslim faith against others, it can be performed using anything from legal,

diplomatic and economic to political means. If there is no peaceful alternative, Islam also allows the use of force, but there are strict rules of engagement. Innocent people such as women, children, or invalids - must never be harmed, and any peaceful offers to stop any further bloodshed from the enemy must be accepted.

Military action is therefore only one means of jihad, and is very rare. To highlight this point, the Prophet Mohammed told his followers returning from a military campaign: "*This day we have returned from the minor jihad to the major jihad.*" What he was saying was that on returning from armed combat in battle they would now be in the battle for self-control and betterment. If military action appears necessary, not everyone can declare jihad. A religious, military campaign must be declared by a proper authority, advised by scholars, who say the religion and people are under threat and violence is imperative to defend them. The concept of "a just war" is very important.

The concept of jihad has been hijacked by many political and religious groups over the ages in a bid to justify various forms of violence. They have twisted and miss used the term to justify military action or various atrocities against innocent civilians. In most cases, Islamic splinter groups invoked jihad to fight against the established Islamic order. Examples of sanctioned military jihad include the Muslims' defensive battles against the Crusaders in medieval times. Therefore, Islamic State are nothing more than a terror group using a twisted religious context to justify their actions.

THIRTEEN - OBSERVATION

Under cloudy skies, we dismounted our DPVs and realised we were must detour around a rebel position, the last thing we wanted was to get drawn into any form of confrontation with another rebel force. Syria was more politically charged than Iraq in many ways. Iraq, we had full governmental support, Syria is a very different prospect. The Assad regime and the civil war is something the U.S. does not want to get directly involved with. Taking sides could lead to further issues with Russia or be seen by the world community as interfering. Our objective in Syria was to only target Islamic State and then leave the country the rebel forces and government to it. Islamic State has used the civil war as a platform to take control over parts of the country.

The Syrian civil war began with the build-up began early spring of 2011 with nationwide protests against President Bashar al-Assad's government, whose forces responded with violent crackdowns. March 15-21, 2011, is considered to be the beginning of the Syrian uprising. On March 18, the protests turned bloody when the Syrian government reacted with deadly violence. Then on 20 March in Daraa after security forces opened fire on the protesting crowd, protesters burned the local Ba'ath Party headquarters, the town's courthouse and a telephone company building. That day 15 demonstrators and 7 policemen were killed in Daraa. As things escalated so did the number of deaths with the death toll at 90 civilians and 7 policemen by March 25, 2011.

The demands of those in the uprising, up until the beginning of April was about democratic reforms, release of political prisoners, "freedom", abolition of emergency law and an end to corruption. This then turned towards the overthrowing of the Assad regime.

As protests spread across Syria so did the violence and military intervention. On April 25, 2011, the Syrian Army started a series of large-scale military attacks on towns, using tanks, infantry carriers, and artillery, to try and curb the ever more violent protests, which lead to hundreds of civilians dying. Assad, in his March 2011 speech addressed the protests. He claimed that an international terrorist conspiracy sought to topple his government. During this time, Assad decided to release extremists from the Sednaya prison; extremists with no association to the uprisings. These fighters would then go on to lead militant groups such as ISIS and al-Qaeda affiliate Jabhat al Nusra. Creating further problems not only for the rebels but the Assad regime and multiple organisations tried to wrangle control of Syria.

We made a diversion of a couple of miles round the rebel force and managed to pass unnoticed, much to our relief. However, this had manged to consume precious mission time.

We had a set area to use as an observation post and capture valuable intelligence on an Islamic State training camp. Drones could only gather so much intelligence and over a set period of time. Often Islamic State would take cover from drones trying to hide their operations. Eyes on the ground over several hours or even better several days could yield a much more accurate picture of what was happening at the location. We could also often better identify who was there and what the area was being used for. If needed, we could also guide in bombing runs on live targets before they could move or hide from coalition aircraft.

We reached our OP at dawn on a rocky outcrop overlooking the Islamic State training camp. Intelligence and aerial photographs showed an uninhabited area, but in fact it was surrounded by Syrian Army forces on one side and an opposing Islamic State force on the other. The SAS also had a patrol out not too far from our location looking at another area believed to be a training camp.

Once at our OP we set up who was going to be on sentry whilst others rested. As Dawn broke the training camp came into view. What looked like a patrol left through the camp gates and headed out on the pack of three pickup trucks. They had a mixture of weapons including an RPD light machine gun which was developed in the Soviet Union in 1945 by Vasily Degtyaryov for the intermediate 7.62x39mm M43 cartridge. A couple of RPGs, PKs and AK-47s were being carried by the rest of the patrol. It was most likely heading off to try to hold back the Syrian government forces.

We continued to observe the training camp for the next twenty-four hours and watch young recruits going through their basic training. Which seemed very basic, half of them seemed unable to fire off an AK-47 without either flying backwards or dropping the weapon in the process. It did make us all smile then Marc said "You know what Islamic State training sucks." Marc was right. Although through being high on drugs or simply dedicated to their cause lack of talent was made up for by sheer aggression.

With all the intelligence, we required captured and passed on. Most likely for air attack we gathered up all out kit to make our way back out of Syria and got mounted up on our DVPs after a short work the where we had concealed them.

We would use the same route that we had used to come in on and avoid any of the opposing forces. The training camp was not one of the larger camps - more of a small training camp with around one hundred personnel. After a couple of hours of driving we were back in Turkey for the usual debrief before chow, rest and preparation for the next operation we would be sent on.

FOURTEEN - LOSS

Iraq October 2015

On October 21, 2015, a raid was launched just east of the Islamic State stronghold of Hawija, in northern Iraq, in the largely Kurdish region of Kirkuk. The mission objective was to rescues 70 hostages being held by Islamic State, due to be executed on the same day as the operation. The prison itself was quite formidable. It was a large compound with bar concrete walls and the floor was strewn with rubble. Delta along with some Peshmerga soldiers would mount an assault to free the prisoners. American led air strikes would bomb the surrounding roads to stop the IS fighters from escaping with any prisoners and leaving them no choice but to fight.

Everyone knew it was a dangerous mission – there are very few which are not. But due to the building and numbers of IS fighters this would be more dangerous than normal. The force consisted of 30 Delta operators and 48 Peshmerga from the Counter Terror Department (CTD). They were flown in by three Chinook Helicopters and three Pave Hawks. The prison was located 4 miles north of Hawija. At 0200 hours, the helicopters began to airdrop the force directly onto the target. The initial plan was for the Peshmerga to lead and Delta to act as fire support. However, almost as soon as the forces had been inserted an intense firefight ensued.

The firefight started as soon as forces got close to the prison. The Peshmerga CTD soldiers soon became pinned down with fire from the prison and Delta had to push forward also coming under fire. Once Delta had made it into the prison. They began room by room clearance. Using night vision goggles each step had to be fought for. IS fighters barefoot and in long robes, some badly stained ran in and out of rooms spraying bullets indiscriminately as they shouted out the locations of Delta and CTD soldier's. Whilst telling each other to "move quickly." In some of the rooms groups of prisoners were huddled together with fear in their eyes. About twenty of them were ex-members of Iraqi security forces. They had been told it was the last day they would be alive and had earlier had to dig their own graves.

These prisoners were pulled out patted down to check they were not IS fighters pretending to be prisoners. Some IS fighters did surrender and were promptly taken prisoner. As well as securing the prisoners the usual process of gathering intelligence was also undertaken.

The bitter firefight continued as Delta made its way through the prison. Taking out IS fighters as they went. After the intense firefight bullet holes, could be seem on most of the walls, although some may have been from earlier battles in and around the compound. Garish bright red and cream stripped wallpaper adorned some of the rooms used as living quarters and offices by the IS fighters. Again, cell phones and laptops were seized in the hope they would yield yet more vital intelligence about Islamic State operations in Iraq. The operation lasted two hours. Master Sergeant Joshua Wheeler had been hit. His face was gray and his eyes were dilating from blood loss and the resulting shock. He was quickly carried to the awaiting helicopters to take him and the rest of the team back to base.

During the raid six IS fighters were killed along with a further 20 wounded.

Four Peshmerga soldiers from the organised local Kurdish Militia were wounded during the fierce firefight that ensued. This raid also sadly, saw the loss of the first American soldier in operations against Islamic State and the first American soldier to die in Iraq in four years. Master Sergeant Joshua Wheeler was shot during the raid and later died from his injuries on October 22 2015, despite the best efforts of medical staff. Bringing home the real danger Special Forces face mounting a war against fanatics. He had followed his training and to ensure that the mission was a success pushed forward into the prison running towards the sound of gunfire. He was then hit by small arms fire losing his life.

Joshua L. Wheeler was born on 22 November 1975 in Roland, Oklahoma. He was a was a highly decorated Delta operator having earned 11 Bronze Star Medals including four with Valor Devices. Wheeler joined the U.S. Army in May 1995 as an infantryman and completed his basic training at Fort Benning, Georgia. Wheeler was then stationed at Fort Lewis, Washington and assigned to Company C, 1st Battalion, 24th Infantry Regiment until 1997 when he was assigned to Company B, 2nd Battalion, 75th Ranger Regiment.

In total Wheeler was deployed three times in support of combat operations to Afghanistan and Iraq with the 75th Ranger Regiment. Wheeler joined Delta in 2004 deploying to Afghanistan and Iraq 11 times to support various operations. The real sad element is that he leaves behind his wife and four children. Three of his children were from his first marriage. His current wife Ashley Wheeler having only given birth to his fourth son in May 2015.

Wheeler had paid the ultimate price to rescue and protect the innocent. In war people die on all sides. However, for those left behind it is of little comfort. All we can do is ensure that the memories of Wheeler and the sacrifices he made for his beloved country never die.

FIFTEEN – END IN SIGHT?

The 'Unit' has been on a constant war footing since it was formed in the 1970s. Some of their achievements prior to 9/11 include the rescue of the American Kurt Kurt Muse from Carcel Modelo prison, Panama City as part of Operation Acid Gambit in 1989 aiding in the elimination of the Columbian drug lord Pablo Escobar. Another unknown, role is in the British SAS and Para rescue of several British soldiers in Sierra Leone as part of Operation Barras in 2000. A day prior to the invasion of Iraq in 2003 Delta Operator's would make their way out of a secret Saudi base called Ar'ar and across the border into Iraq as the first invasion force to enter. They flew across the desert at speed in 15 Swiss made Pinzgauers high-mobility all-terrain 4×4 and 6×6 military utility vehicles. Accompanied by a pair of SUVs with a reconnaissance drone flying above.

They then undertook devastating night-time raids as a diversion and to panic the Iraqi forces into thinking a much larger invasion force from the west was now inside Iraq. In 2004, Delta Force took part in both the First and Second Battles of Fallujah in Iraq. Delta's role in the earlier first Battle of Fallujah - Operation Vigilant Resolve in April 2004. Master Sgt. Don Hollenbaugh and Staff Sgt. Dan Briggs were awarded the Distinguished Service Cross for their actions as a small Delta element fought alongside a Marine platoon on April 26, 2004. The combined Delta and Marine force consisted of 30 Marines and seven Delta operators. They quickly found themselves heavily engaged by an estimated 300 insurgents. Medic Briggs exposed himself to enemy fire on multiple occasions, sprinting back and forth between two buildings to treat wounded Marines. Hollenbaugh, meanwhile, held off the attack from a compound roof. He then continued to hold off the attack single-handedly for quite a while after Delta operators and the Marines had evacuated the immediate area. He intentionally skipped bullets off walls and floors to get at otherwise unreachable enemy fighters, ducked under a rocket-propelled grenade, rolled into a stairway to avoid being hit by the shrapnel of a grenade tossed onto the roof, and rapidly switched positions to appear to be more than just a one-man defensive element. He used all his available skill and training to keep a tenacious and numerically enemy force at bay. During the Invasion of Iraq and subsequent raids to locate key Iraqi personnel, including Saddam Hussein and running battles with pockets of resistance in intense battles. It is believed over half of Delta's operators were wounded.

Romantizing about war is not something that this book has been intended to portray. I have written this book to try and show the bravery, courage and skill of a bunch of highly skilled and highly trained individuals. In war people die on all sides – families loose loved ones be it friend or foe. The hardest part of the job I do is the loss of a fellow operator. Often these are individuals who are not only young and in their prime, but also individuals with whom you form a different kind of bond. You just do not form bonds like that in normal life. These bonds are formed from what you go through together often relying on one another to stay alive. When they are taken away it is like losing a family member - a fellow brother. It does take a little piece of you away each it happens and without a doubt and changes you. Those that have fought in any war zone have gone through the same mixture of feelings I have gone through. Although, my experiences are not even close to what those in World War I or II went through.

Being in combat does change how you view the world especially after you have watched people die. The small things that stress people out at home such as losing their cell phone or being late for an important meeting seem so insignificant to me. These things don't really wreck your day; they are merely an inconvenience. Seeing the aftermath of a father being killed in front of his wife and children, a child left without a family after everyone else has been killed. Innocent civilians being needlessly slaughtered. Those are the kind of things that wreck your day. Those are the things that have brought me the most sadness and made me wonder why we must have war in the first place. I now know more than ever; my job is to do anything and everything I can in my small way to stop this happening. Killing people is far easier than I thought it would be. However, those that I have killed have often either conducted or planned to conduct evil acts on innocent people. That for me is enough to justify removing them from this world. They have no intention of changing – they are focused on chaos and destruction. Some of these have become evil through power or money. Using it to inflict brutality on other individuals. I doubt I will go to heaven, but who knows my sins may be forgiven. That is up to God, but for now whilst I am still on this earth. I can only try to ensure, I keep my family and my beloved country safe and out of harm's way. For that I make no apologies…

As I write this (April 2016) the coalition has trained six Iraqi brigades. These have been called the Mosul Counterattack Brigades or just the Counterattack Brigades. These Counterattack brigades did most of the work at Ramadi and they are now being moved north to begin the removal of Islamic State in Mosul where it all began. These coalition trained forces have had input from Delta and are now outperforming brigades that have not receive any coalition training. It has helped lift morale and given the Iraqi government more faith in the U.S. presence in Iraq. Air strikes have stepped up and almost carpet bombing an area before Iraqi forces mount an attack has been found to hit Islamic State even harder. With a greater targeting of deliberate targets such as Islamic State oil, money, bomb-making plants, weapons storage and transportation. This combined with judicious use of special forces has increased the rate at which Islamic State are being suppressed and almost surgically removed from Iraq. To aid in this, extra assets have been deployed such as the tube artillery deployed to Makhmur and advanced multiple-rocket launcher systems that have been employed in other parts of Iraq. With this IS Fighters moral especially in Fallujah and Mosul is starting to waver. Their commanders fear they no longer have the same will to either fight or defend that they once had. With a movement of some recruits and experienced fighters to Libya.

Iraqi forces are pushing at a reasonable pace towards Qayyarah West airfield, west of the Tigris River south of Mosul. Qayyarah West can then serve as a logistical hub and staging base for a more deliberate assault toward Mosul somewhat later. At the current rate of progress Mosul should be recaptured and Islamic State pretty much ejected from Iraq within the next twelve months.

For Iraq to stabilize though this means that its political state needs to be addressed so that military success can lead to political achievements and prevent a re-occurrence. It must not be forgotten that Islamic State are the ones holding together various Iraqi groups. This could potentially lead to the same cycle of events post the invasion of Iraq in 2003 leading Iraq to fall back into civil war. In effect this could potentially mean that all this military intervention has been undertaken in vain. With the removal of Islamic State either through them being destroyed or deciding to flee. It could potentially lead to another Iraqi group deciding to take control of parts of Mosul. This could then lead to further conflict between various Iraqi groups all vying for control. Effectively solving one problem for another to take its place.

Iraqi security forces would have to take control quickly and ensure it had the political solutions to finally bring stability and an element of peace to those living in and around Mosul.

Another critical political-military problem is the question of the Hashd ash-Shaabi group. Prime Minister Haider al-Abadi understands their importance, especially as they were the ones who halted the Islamic State offensive on Baghdad in 2014. They also have the potential to undermine Iraqi security forces due to being an Iranian-backed alternative military force.

One plan is to integrate Hashd personnel into Iraqi forces something Hashd ash-Shaabi commanders have suggested they will do. The government's idea was to essentially pay the Hashd and control them through the use of payment. If conscription was brought in this may help the matter further. As the Israelis demonstrated in 1948. They found that military service was a powerful method of socialization. The Iraqi military personnel is carefully looking at and considering the Israeli model to think about how Iraq might use conscription to help heal the rifts and build a new, unified Iraqi society. It remains to be seen if this will solve or reduce the issues within Iraq. Although, Iraq is at least still several years away from being able to implement conscription. During that time and the Hashd could continue to destabilize and undermine Iraq and decide that it does not want to be integrated into Iraq. The next twelve months may well be the most critical phase of the war against Islamic State...

GLOSSARY

AK-47 – The AK47 Kalashnikov assault rifle is more commonly known as the AK-47 or just AK (Avtomat Kalashnikova – 47, which translates to the Kalashnikov automatic rifle, model 1947), and its derivatives. It had been and still is with minor modifications, manufactured in dozens of countries, and has been used in hundreds of countries and conflicts since its introduction. The total number of the AK-type rifles made worldwide during the last 60 years is estimated at 90+ million. The AK47 is known for its simplicity of operation, ruggedness and maintenance, and unsurpassed reliability even in the most inhospitable of conditions.

Apache AH-64 – The Boeing Apache AH-64 is a twin engine four blade attack helicopter with a tailwheel-type landing gear arrangement, and a tandem cockpit for a two-man crew. It features a nose-mounted sensor suite for target acquisition and night vision systems. It is armed with a 30 mm M230 chain gun carried between the main landing gear, under the aircraft's forward fuselage. It has four hardpoints mounted on stub-wing pylons, typically carrying a mixture of AGM-114 Hellfire missiles and Hydra 70 rocket pods. The Apache entered U.S. Army service in April 1986. The first production AH-64D, an upgraded Apache variant, was delivered to the Army in March 1997. Over 2,000 AH-64s have been produced to date with the latest AH-64E. With an AH-64F Apache concept being revealed in 2014.

AV8B – The AV8B was manufactured under licence by McDonnell Douglas and based on the Hawker Sidney Harrier jump jet and later AV8A. Capable of vertical or short takeoff and landing (V/STOL), the aircraft was designed in the late 1970s as an Anglo-American development of the British Hawker Siddeley Harrier. It first flew in 1978 and is powered by a single Rolls-Royce F402-RR-408 (Mk 107) vectored-thrust turbofan. The AV8B is based on the Harrier two, and produced jointly McDonnell Douglas and British Aerospace. The UK Harrier fleet was retired from service in 2010.

B1-B – The Rockwell now Boeing B-1B bomber is a four engine heavy strategic supersonic bomber. It was first envisioned in the 1960s as a supersonic swept wing bomber with Mach 2 speed, and sufficient range and payload to replace the Boeing B-52 Stratofortress. It was developed into the B-1B, primarily a low-level penetrator with long range and Mach 1.25 speed capability at high altitude. It bets the nickname 'Bone' from originally being called the B-One. The initial B-1A version was developed in the early 1970s, but its production was cancelled, and only four prototypes were built. The need for a new platform once again surfaced in the early 1980s, and the aircraft resurfaced as the B-1B version with the focus on low-level penetration bombing. However, by this point, development of stealth technology was promising an aircraft of dramatically improved capability. Production went ahead as the B version would be operational before the new generation of steal bombers. It first flew in December 1974 and entered service in 1986. Powered by four General Electric F101-GE-102 augmented turbofans with 14,600 lbf thrust. With a top speed of Mach 1.25 at high altitude and Mach 0.92 at low altitude. With a range of 5,900 miles and can carry 75,000 pounds of internal ordnance and 50,000 pounds on six external hardpoints.

B-52 – The Boeing B-52 bomber is a long-range, subsonic, jet-powered strategic bomber. The B-52 was designed and built by Boeing, which has continued to provide support and upgrades. It has been operated by the United States Air Force since the 1950s. It has seen action in numerous war zones and has been updated several times during is a long service history. The B-52 completed sixty years of continuous service with its original operator in 2015. After being upgraded between 2013 and 2015, it is expected to serve into the 2040s. Powered by eight Pratt & Whitney TF33-P-3/103 turbofans ach with an output of 17,000 lbf. It has a maximum speed of 650 mph and a range of 4,480 miles. It can carry 70,000 lb of mixed ordnance.

Bell Boeing V-22 Opsrey - The V-22 Osprey is a multi-mission, tiltrotor military aircraft with both a vertical takeoff and landing (VTOL), and short takeoff and landing (STOL) capability. It was designed to combine the functionality of a conventional helicopter with the long-range, high-speed cruise performance of a turboprop aircraft. The V-22 originated from the United States Department of Defense Joint-service Vertical take-off/landing Experimental (JVX) aircraft program started in 1981. The team of Bell Helicopter and Boeing Helicopters was awarded a development contract in 1983 for the tiltrotor aircraft. The Bell Boeing team jointly produce the aircraft. The V-22 first flew in 1989, and began flight testing and design alterations; the complexity and difficulties of being the first tiltrotor intended for military service in the world led to many years of development. The V-22 entered service with the U.S. Marines in 2007. It is powered by two Rolls-Royce Allison T406/AE 1107C-Liberty turboshafts, each producing 6,150 hp with a top speed of 351mph and a range of 1011 miles.

BLU-82B - The BLU-82B/C-130 weapon system, known under program "Commando Vault" and nicknamed "daisy cutter" in Vietnam and in Afghanistan for its ability to flatten a forest into a helicopter landing zone. It was a 15,000-pound conventional bomb, delivered from either a C-130 or an MC-130 transport aircraft. It was retired in 2008.

BMP-1 - The BMP-1 is a Soviet amphibious tracked infantry fighting vehicle. BMP stands for Boyevaya Mashina Pekhoty 1 meaning "infantry fighting vehicle". The BMP-1 was the first mass-produced infantry fighting vehicle (IFV) of USSR. It was called the M-1967, BMP and BMP-76PB by NATO before its correct designation was known. The Soviet military leadership saw any future wars as being conducted with nuclear, chemical and biological weapons and a new design combining the properties of an armoured personnel carrier (APC) and a light tank like the BMP would allow the infantry to operate from the relative safety of its armoured, radiation-shielded interior in contaminated areas and to fight alongside it in uncontaminated areas. It would increase infantry squad mobility, provide fire support to them, and also be able to fight alongside main battle tanks

E-3 Sentry - The E-3 Sentry, commonly known as AWACS, is an airborne early warning and control (AEW&C) aircraft developed by Boeing as the prime contractor. Derived from the Boeing 707 320B Advanced, which entered commercial airline service in 1962 and stayed in production until the end of 707 production in 1979. AWACS provides all-weather surveillance, command, control and communications, and is used by the United States Air Force (USAF), NATO, Royal Air Force (RAF), French Air Force and Royal Saudi Air Force. The E-3 is distinguished by the distinctive black and white rotating radar dome above the fuselage. Powered by four Pratt and Whitney TF33-PW-100A turbofans, with a range of 4600 miles and a 530 mph top speed. It was produced between 1977 and 1992 with a total of 68 having been made. Long term the Boing 767 will be equipped with the same package as the Boeing 707. The current AWACS is planned to stay in service until 2050 with several upgrades and refurbishments.

DShK – The DShK is a Russian heavy machine gun that came into service in 1938. It is gas operated, with a 12.7x109 mm calibre belt fed and air cooled machine gun. It can be used as an anti-aircraft gun mounted on a pintle. It is also easily mounted to trucks or other vehicles as an infantry heavy support weapon.

Eurofighter Typhoon – The Typhoon is a multirole, twin engine supersonic fighter with a canard-delta wing. It was designed and built by a European tri-consortium of Alenia Aermacchi, Airbus Group and BAE Systems. Political issues in the partner nations significantly protracted the Typhoon's development; the sudden end of the Cold War reduced European demand for fighter aircraft, and there was debate over the cost and work share of the Eurofighter. The Typhoon first flew on March 27, 2004 and entered service on August 4, 2003. It is powered by two Eurojet EJ200 afterburning turbofans. With a top speed of Mach two and the ability to supercruise up to Mack 1.5. It has a combat range of up to 860 miles with three drop tanks.

General Dynamics F-16 'Fighting Falcon' – The F-16 is a single engine supersonic, multirole fighter aircraft, developed for the USAF. It first flew in January 1974 and is powered by a single F110-GE-100 afterburning turbofan engine. It is one of the most manoeuvrable aircraft in the world and is used by the U.S. Air Force Thunderbirds display team and has been exported to quite a few air forces around the world.

JSOC – JSOC (Joint Special Operations Command) is an element of the United States Special Operations Command (USSOCOM) and is charged with the study of special operations requirements and techniques to ensure interoperability and equipment standardization; plan and conduct special operations exercises and training; develop joint special operations tactics; and execute special operations missions worldwide. It was established in 1980 on recommendation of Colonel Charlie Beckwith, in the aftermath of the ill-fated Operation Eagle Claw – See Appendix II

LAW - The M72 LAW (Light Anti-Tank Weapon, also referred to as the Light Anti-Armor Weapon or LAW as well as LAWS Light Anti-Armor Weapons System) is a portable one-shot 66 mm unguided anti-tank weapon. The most common M72A2 LAWs came prepacked with a rocket containing a 66 mm HEAT warhead which is attached to the inside of the launcher by the igniter. It has an effective range of 660ft.

Lockheed C130 Hercules – The Lockheed C130 Hercules is a four engine turboprop transport aircraft with a high wing design. It first flew in August 1954. Since then there have been many variants used by over 70 countries around the world. Originally powered by four 4

Allison T56-A-15 turboprops. It can carry a payload of around 20,000 kg or up to 92 passengers. It is a highly versatile aircraft and has seen use across the world over its 50 years of continuous service.

Lockheed C-141 Starlifter: The Lockheed C-141 Starlifter was a military strategic airlifter in service with the Military Air Transport Service (MATS), its successor organization the Military Airlift Command (MAC), and finally the Air Mobility Command (AMC) of the United States Air Force (USAF). Introduced to replace slower piston-engine cargo planes such as the C-124 Globemaster II, the C-141 was designed to requirements set in 1960 and first the C-141 first flew in 1963. Production deliveries of an eventual 285 planes began in 1965. 284 for the Air Force, and one for the National Aeronautics and Space Administration (NASA) for use as an airborne observatory. The aircraft remained in service for over 40 years until the USAF withdrew the last C-141s from service in 2006, after replacing the C-141 with the C-17 Globemaster III. The C-141 was powered by four Pratt & Whitney TF33-P-7 turbofans, developing 20,250 lbf of thrust each. It had a top speed of 567 mph and a range of 2.935 miles.

McDonnell Douglas (Now Boeing) F15E 'Strike Eagle' – The F15E Strike Eagle is an all-weather multirole fighter, derived from the McDonnell Douglas (now Boeing) F-15 Eagle. It is powered by two Pratt & Whitney F100-229 afterburning turbofans, 29,000 lbf and capable of Mach 2.5 (2.5 the speed of sound). It first flew in December 1986 and an F15SG version is on order by the ordered by the Republic of Singapore Air Force (RSAF).

Humvee – The HMMWV (High Mobility Multipurpose Wheeled Vehicle), commonly known as the Humvee, is an American four-wheel drive military vehicle produced by AM General. It has largely supplanted the roles formerly served by smaller Jeeps. It has been in service since 1984 and served in all theatres of war. Powered by an 8 Cylinder. Diesel 6.2 L or 6.5 L V8 turbo diesel and with a top speed of over 70 mph, which drops to 55mph when loaded up to its gross weight. It initially lacked any armour, but later version has had some armour protection added against small arms fire.

M4 Carbine - The M4 carbine is a family of firearms that are originally based on earlier carbine versions of the M16 rifle. The M4 is a shorter and lighter variant of the M16A2 assault rifle, allowing its user to better operate in close quarters combat. It has 80% parts commonality with the M16A2. It is a gas-operated, magazine-fed, selective fire, shoulder-fired weapon with a telescoping stock. Like the rest of the M16 family, it fires the standard .223 caliber, or 5.56mm NATO round.

M16 – The M16 is a lightweight, 5.56 mm, air-cooled, gas-operated, magazine-fed assault rifle, with a rotating bolt, actuated by direct impingement gas operation. The rifle is made of steel, 7075 aluminium alloy, composite plastics and polymer materials. It was developed from the AR-15 and came into service in 1963. The M16 is now the most commonly manufactured 5.56x45 mm rifle in the world. Currently the M16 is in service with more than 80 countries worldwide. It has grown a reputation for ruggedness and reliability and was adopted by the SAS over the less reliable SA80. Later the SAS adopted the C8

Panavia Tornado GR4 - The Panavia Tornado is a family of twin-engine, variable-sweep wing combat aircraft, which was jointly developed and manufactured by Italy, the United Kingdom, and West Germany. There are three primary Tornado variants: The Tornado IDS (Interdictor/strike) fighter-bomber, the suppression of enemy air defences Tornado ECR (electronic combat/reconnaissance) and the Tornado ADV (air defence variant) interceptor aircraft. The Tornado ADV variant is no longer in RAF service having been retired in 2011, being replaced by the Typhoon. Powered by two Turbo-Union RB199-34R Mk 103 afterburning turbofans and a top speed of Mach 2.2. It has proved to be a very successful aircraft and still in front line service. The Tornado was developed and built by Panavia Aircraft GmbH, a trinational consortium consisting of British Aerospace (previously British Aircraft Corporation), MBB of West Germany, and Aeritalia of Italy. It first flew on 14 August 1974 and was introduced into service in 1979–1980.

PK - The Kalashnikov PK is a 7.62 mm general-purpose machine gun designed in the Soviet Union. The PK machine gun was introduced in the 1960s and replaced the SGM and RP-46 machine guns in Soviet service. It remains in use as a front-line infantry and vehicle-mounted weapon with Russia's armed forces, and has been exported extensively. It can fire at 650-750 rounds a minute from belts in 100/200/250 round boxes. Fired from the ground from either a Bi-pod or tripod and an effective range of 1,500m.

Pave Hawk – The Sikorsky HH-60 Pave Hawk is a twin turboshaft engine helicopter and a derivative of the UH-60 Black Hawk. The MH-60G Pave Hawk's is the insertion and recovery of special operations personnel. The HH-60G version is the recovery of personnel under stressful conditions, including search and rescue. Both versions conduct day or night operations into hostile environments. It features an upgraded communications and navigation suite that includes an integrated inertial navigation/global positioning/Doppler navigation systems, satellite communications, secure voice, and Have Quick communications. The term PAVE stands for Precision Avionics Vectoring Equipment. All HH-60Gs have an automatic flight control system, night vision goggles lighting and forward looking infrared system that greatly enhances night low-level operations. Additionally, some Pave Hawks have color weather radar and an engine/rotor blade anti-ice system that gives the HH-60G an all-weather capability. Pave Hawk mission equipment includes a retractable in-flight refuelling probe, internal auxiliary fuel tanks, two crew-served (or pilot-controlled) 7.62 mm miniguns or .50-caliber machine guns and an 8,000-pound capacity cargo hook. To improve air transportability and shipboard operations, all HH-60Gs have folding rotor blades.

RC-135 Rivet Joint – The Boeing RC-135 is based C-135 Stratolifter airframe, and is a four engine wept wing intelligence gathering plane, used by the United States Air Force. More recently three have been purchased by three RAF to replace the Nimrod R1 and MR1. The C-135 is essentially a military version of the Boeing 707 and first flew on 17 August 1957. The RC-135 was ordered in 1962 and was a modified version of the C-135A. A total of nine were originally ordered. In total there is currently 32 in operation, including the first delivery to the RAF. The RAF version is the latest RC-135W Joint River, converted from KC-135R airframes first delivered in 1964. Powered by four CFM International F-108-CF-201 turbofan engines, producing 22,000 lbf (96 kN) each. They are the same engines as used on the current Boeing 737 800.

RPD Light Machine Gun is an automatic weapon using a gas-operated long stroke piston system and a locking system recycled from previous Degtyaryov small arms, consisting of a pair of hinged flaps set in recesses on each side of the receiver. It fires 7.62 mm ammunition from a cylindrical metal container that clips on and holds 100 rounds. It can fire 650-750 rounds per minute is an effective ire support weapon. For firing from the prone position, as well as adding stability when firing, a bipod is fitted to the front of the weapon.

The RPG-7 is a portable, unguided, shoulder-launched, anti-tank rocket-propelled grenade launcher. Originally the RPG-7 and its predecessor, the RPG-2, were designed by the Soviet Union. The ruggedness, simplicity, low cost, and effectiveness of the RPG-7 has made it the most widely used anti-armour weapon in the world. Currently around 40 countries use the weapon, and it is manufactured in a number of variants by nine countries. The RPG has been used in almost all conflicts across all continents since the mid-1960s from the Vietnam War to the early 2010s War in Afghanistan.

Sikorsky MH-53 - The Sikorsky MH-53 Pave Low series is a long-range combat search and rescue (CSAR) helicopter for the United States Air Force. The series was upgraded from the HH-53B/C, variants of the Sikorsky CH-53 Sea Stallion. The HH-53 "Super Jolly Green Giant" was initially developed to replace the HH-3 "Jolly Green Giant". The helicopters later transitioned to Special Operations missions. The MH-53J Pave Low III helicopter was the largest, most powerful and technologically advanced transport helicopter in the US Air Force inventory. The terrain-following and terrain-avoidance radar, forward looking infrared sensor, inertial navigation system with Global Positioning System, along with a projected map display enable the crew to follow terrain contours and avoid obstacles, making low-level penetration possible. Powered by two T64-GE-100 turboshaft, 4,330 shp each a top speed of 196 and a range of 680 miles.

Sikorsky UH-60 Black Hawk – The UH-60 Black Hawk has been cemented in history after the books and film 'Black hawk down'. It is a four bladed twin engine medium lift helicopter designed for the United States Army. It first flew in October 1974 and has been used in a variety of roles and variants since then. Powered by two General Electric T700-GE-701C turboshaft, engines it can carry a variety of payloads and be adapted to suit a wide variety of missions. It was designed from the outset to a high survivability on the battlefield. First being used in combat during the invasion of Grenada in 1983.

T-62 is a Soviet main battle tank produced between 1961 and 1975. It became a standard tank in the Soviet arsenal, partly replacing the T-55, although that tank continued to be manufactured in the Soviet Union and elsewhere after T-62 production had ceased. The T-62 was later replaced in front-line service by the T-72. Powered by a V-55 12-cylinder, 4-stroke one-chamber 38.88 litre water-cooled diesel engine, developing 581hp. The T-62 has a top speed of 31 mph on the road and 25 mph cross country.

T-72 is a second generation tank entering service in 1973 and went on to become the most common tank used by the Warsaw pact. Its basic design has been used in the T-90. It weighs 41 tons and has a 125 mm 2A46M smoothbore gun, 7.62 mm PKT coax machine gun and 12.7 mm NSVT antiaircraft machine gun. Powered by a V-12 diesel, with 780 hp and a top speed of 37 mph. Over 25,000 have been produced so far and it currently remains in production.

ZSU-23-2 – The ZU-23-2 "Sergey" is a Soviet towed 23 mm anti-aircraft twin-barrelled autocannon. It was designed to engage low-flying targets at a range of 2.5 km as well as armoured vehicles, at a range of 2 km and for direct defence of troops and strategic locations against air assault usually conducted by helicopters and low-flying airplanes. Normally, once each barrel has fired 100 rounds, it becomes too hot and is therefore replaced with a spare barrel.

APPENDIX I
THE BIRTH OF DELTA

Charles Beckwith was the father of Delta Force not only having the idea but also being the one who brought Delta to life. Beckwith began his military career after being commissioned as a Second Lieutenant in the U.S. Army in 1952. After the end of the Korean War, Beckwith served as a Platoon Leader with Charlie Company, 17th Infantry Regiment and 7th Infantry Division in the Republic of Korea. In 1955, Beckwith was assigned to the 82nd Airborne Division as the commander of the combat support company of the 504th Parachute Infantry Regiment. Two years later, having completed Ranger School, Beckwith joined the Special Forces, and in 1960 was deployed to South Vietnam and Laos as a military advisor.

It was his time as an exchange officer with the SAS that he picked up on the SAS capability and realized that America needed a similar type of force. During his time with the SAS he undertook guerrilla operations during the Malayan Emergency. In the jungle, he contracted leptospirosis so severe doctors did not expect him to survive, but he made a full recovery within months. As soon as Beckwith returned from England, he presented a report which was very detailed and outlined the U.S Army's vulnerability in not having a Special Forces capability like the SAS. Beckwith rose to captain and continued to re-submit his report. Each time his idea was rejected as the top brass felt they did not need a completely new unit.

With Beckwith now the 7th Special Forces Group Special Operations Officer, Beckwith decided to revolutionize Green Beret training. At the time, US Special Forces generally focussed on unconventional warfare and supporting internal foreign defense by training internal forces to either overthrow a government or support a government.

Beckwith knew that:

"Before a Special Forces Green Beret soldier could become a good unconventional soldier, he'd first have to be a good conventional one... Because I had commanded rifle and weapons companies, I was appalled on arriving in Special Forces to find officers who had never commanded conventional units."

Beckwith decided to re-write American Special Forces training from what he had learnt from his time with the SAS. Officer's and soldiers' had to earn the right to wear the 'Green Beret' as this was a symbol of 'excellence.' This was the reverse to where previously officers had been given a Green Beret straight out of War College, with no experience and no special forces training. The high standards Beckwith installed, lead towards the birth of the modern Q-course.

In Vietnam, Beckwith commanded a Special Forces unit code-named Project DELTA. Then in 1966 he took a .50 caliber bullet through his abdomen, putting him on the critical list and for the second time, doctors fearing he would die. He pulled through yet again, making a full recovery, before moving to the U.S Army Ranger school in Florida and overhauled their training by changing a particular a scripted World War Two phase into a Vietnam orientated jungle training regime phase.

Lieutenant Colonel Beckwith returned to Vietnam in 1968, taking command of the 2nd Battalion, 327th Infantry (Airborne), 1st Brigade, 101st Airborne Division. The 327th saw many successes under Beckwith's command, including Operation Mingo, Operation Jeb Stuart, and Operation Nevada Eagle. From 1973 to 1974 Beckwith served as Commander, Control Team "B" with the JCRC (Joint Casualty Resolution Center) located at RTAFB Nakhon Phanom, Thailand. He was promoted to Colonel while there. Under the Command of BG Robert C. Kingston, USA, JCRC's sole mission was to assist the Secretaries of the Armed Services to resolve the fate of servicemen still missing and unaccounted for as a result of the hostilities throughout Indochina. JCRC had a predominantly operational role. After this Beckwith was stationed at Fort Bragg, North Carolina, where he commanded training operations.

Although Beckwith had presented proposals throughout the '60s for a new U.S Army Special Forces unit, the idea had sat on the shelf for a decade. Finally, in the mid-'70s, as the threat of international terrorism became imminent, Beckwith was appointed to form his unit. Delta

Force was founded in November 1977 as a counter-terrorist unit based on the model of the British Special Air Service. It had a greater focus though on hostage rescue along with covert operations and specialized reconnaissance. At the time aircraft hijackings had become quite common. Delta Force's first mission, was the ill-fated Operation Eagle Claw (see Chapter Eleven). Following Beckwith's disappointment at the failure of Desert Claw, Beckwith retired from the Army. He started a consulting firm and wrote a book about Delta Force. Beckwith died June 13, 1994 aged 65 of natural causes.

His fledging Delta Force went from strength to strength to become one of the world's finest Special Forces units. Conducting operations in Mogadishu, Iraq, Afgahnistan, and former Yugoslavia along with many others.

Delta Force's structure is quite similar to the British SAS and is based at Fort Bragg

Delta Force is organized into 4 Squadrons:

A Squadron

B Squadron

C Squadron

D Squadron

Each squadron is made up of 2 or 3 Troops consisting of a Recce / Sniper Troop and up to two Direct Action / Assault troops.

APPENDIX II
Operation Desert Claw

The ill-fated Operation Eagle Claw was the very first operation of the newly formed Delta Force. Although the failure of the mission was not of Delta's making. It is akin to saying that a baseball team lost the game because the bus taking them to the game broke down. The operation was arranged by the American president at the time, Jimmy Carter, in response to the Iran hostage crisis, and involved rescuing 52 Americans that had been taken captive at the US Embassy in Tehran. The operation was both a military and political failure. Many errors in the planning led to problems in the execution, especially with the aviation side of the operation. The Joint Task Force commander for the operation was Major General James B Vaught, the fixed-wing and air mission commander was Colonel James H. Kyle, the helicopter commander was Marine Lieutenant Colonel Edward R. Seiffert, and the Delta Force commander were Colonel Charlie Beckwith, a retired US Army Special Forces Officer who was now in charge of the Tehran CIA Special Activities Division paramilitary team. He had been given two assignments; he was to gather information about the hostages, as well as transport the rescue team from Desert Two, the FUP (Forming-Up Point), to the Embassy grounds to stage the actual rescue. The most important intelligence was gathered from the Embassy cook, who had been released by the hostage takers. He revealed that all the hostages were centrally located within the embassy compound, and this would be a key point used in planning the rescue mission.

Three weeks before the operation on April 1, 1980, a US AFCC (Air Force Combat Controller) was flown in to survey the staging area code named Desert One, located in South Khorasan Province of Iran, near Tabas. He was able to fully survey the airstrip and install some remotely controlled infra-red landing lights and a strobe. He also took a soil sample that in the end would prove fruitless. At the time of the survey the desert floor was packed hard, but over the next three weeks an ankle-deep layer of fine sand was deposited on the airstrip by sandstorms.

The whole operation was a complex one and would be staged over two separate nights. The first night would be spent securing Desert One and ensuring 6,000 gallons of aviation fuel that the USAF had brought in was secured. Eight RH-35D Stallion helicopters of the US Marine Corps were due to arrive from the USS Nimitz. These were painted in a desert colour and all markings removed for the operation. The eight helicopters would then be used to transport Delta Force from Desert One to Desert Two. Once at Desert Two, the helicopters, their crews and Delta Force would hide until the next night. On the second night, the actual rescue mission would be mounted. The CIA would bring in trucks to transport Delta Force before driving the trucks containing Delta Force to Tehran. Simultaneously, other US Troops would disable the power in the area close to the embassy. This was intended to slow down any response from the Iranian military's C-130As, with their 20 mm rotary cannons and 40 mm Bofors cannon. The final element was that the army Rangers would capture the nearby Manzariyeh Air Base so that several C-141 Starlifters could arrive for the evacuation of personnel and hostages. Delta Force would assault the Embassy and eliminate the guards. Afterwards, the hostages and Delta Force operatives would rendezvous with the helicopters across the street at the Shahid Shiroudi Stadium. The helicopters would convey everyone back to the C-141s at Manzariyeh Air Base. The operation involved air support via Air Wings 8 operating from USS Nimitz and Air Wings 14 operating from USS Coral Sea.

The rescue team and its equipment, along with fuel, were in MC-130Es, a low level clandestine penetration aircraft suitable for Special Forces operations. It was a modified C130 with the addition of special electronics and a low radar observant paint. The EC-130H was another modified C130 used for Airborne Communications Jamming. Through the failing light a single C-130E moved fast and low over dark waters toward the coast of Iran. It was a big four-propeller U.S. Air Force workhorse, a C-130, painted in a mottled black-and-green camouflage that made it all but invisible against the black water and the night sky. It flew with no lights. Inside there was an eerie red glow from the plane's blackout lamps, seventy-four men struggled to get comfortable in a cramped, unaccommodating space, with essential supplies packed into the hold as well. The C-130E refuelled in mid-air on the way to Desert One by a KC-135 tanker just off the Iranian coast. The C-130E then flew in at 250 feet over the coast of Iran, well below Iranian radar, before it began a gradual climb to 5,000 feet. It was still flying dangerously low, even at that altitude, because the land rose up suddenly, almost in row after row of jagged ridges—the Zagros Mountains, which looked almost jet black in the pilots' night-vision goggles that gave a grey-green tint to everything he viewed. Its terrain-hugging radar was so sensitive that even though the plane was safely above the peaks, the highest ridges triggered a loud, and almost disconcerting sound from the terrain warning system.

The first EC-130E landed at 10:45pm just before, it landed the hidden lights were activated. Other than those lights, the landing was done in a complete blackout. The pilots had night vision goggles in which to see the infra-red landing lights. The first EC-130E call sign, Dragon One, made four passes to ensure there were no obstructions as it was heavily laden and there was a truck trundling along the runway. However, the landing still resulted in substantial wing damage that would require an extensive rebuild, even though the aircraft remained flyable. The soft sand that had covered the hard runway meant the C-130 was enveloped in an almost opaque cloud as it landed and ground to a halt. As soon as it had stopped, the rear ramp was lowered and Rangers roared off in a Jeep and on a motorcycle to give chase to the truck. The tanker truck was smuggling fuel and trying to escape the area. It was soon caught up with and then blown up by a LAW fired by one of the Rangers. The Ranger had not realised it was full of fuel. The subsequent explosion lit up the nighttime sky for miles around and surely alerted the Iranians to the presence of something going on. The explosion and fireball from the tanker aided the landing for the disorientated RH-53D crews that were coming into land, and gave them a strong visual marker. The passenger in the truck was killed instantly, but the driver managed to run away. He was not considered a threat though; due to his involvement in smuggling, it was felt he would not tip off the authorities. Almost at the same time as the tanker had been blown up, an Iranian bus travelled along the runway, which also served as a road. The civilian bus had 43 passengers on board, along with a driver. There was no alternative other than to detain the bus and the passengers until the operation had been completed. The Rangers shot at the bus to disable it, putting a hole in the radiator and bursting a tyre, which presently brought it to a halt. The passengers were offloaded and searched for weapons, before the conclusion was drawn that they were just poor Iranians in the wrong place at the wrong time.

The second and third MC-130Es landed and unloaded their cargo before taking off at 11:15pm to make room for the two EC-130Es to land, along with the 8 RH-53Ds. The assault team that had been brought in consisted of 120 Delta Force operatives along with 12 Rangers and 15 Iranian Americas who would drive the trucks.

The RH-53Ds were given the call sign Bluebeard and then a number between one and eight. One of the RH-53Ds was lost on the way as a warning light came on for a sensor that the pilot interpreted as a cracked rotor blade. The helicopter was left in the desert and its crew picked up by Bluebeard 8. The helicopters continued on before running into unexpected weather in the form of a haboob, a dust storm in which fine sand particles become suspended in the air. Bluebeard 5 suffered erratic flight instrumentation controls after flying into the haboob and had to abort, returning to USS Nimitz as non-visual flying became impossible. Finally, what was left of the now scattered formation of RH-53Ds arrived at Desert One. Bluebeard 2 arrived with a malfunction in its second stage hydraulics system, leaving only the primary system with which to fly the aircraft. Out of the eight helicopters, which were sent to the first staging area, Desert One, only five managed to arrive in an operational condition. With only five, the minimum needed to complete the mission had been met. One of the helicopters on landing, had hit a rut, which had in turn burst a rear tyre causing it to come off the rim of the wheel. The decision to abort was already being discussed by the various commanders who were unable to fully make a decision. There was a refusal to use Bluebeard 2 and then a refusal to reduce the size of the Delta Force team. There was the feeling that more helicopters would be lost to failure. One issue with the RH-53D was its notorious ability to fail on cold starts. The EC-130s had used an extra 90 minutes of fuel whilst idling on the ground, although the thought was that since only six helicopters would arrive, there would be more fuel available. 1,000 US gallons could be transferred from the fuel bladders. However, it was found that one of the EC-130s had used all the fuel in its bladder in refuelling just three helicopters, meaning there would be no spare once all six were refuelled. The recommendation to abort was also passed on to the President. Without this extra fuel, the EC-130 needed to leave immediately to ensure it was able to make it to the KC-135 tanker. Bluebeard 3 was currently blocking its path and also needed to be moved so it could be refuelled on the opposite side of the runway.

Bluebeard 3 was unable to move by ground taxi so it was decided the only way to move it was by hover taxi. Using the Combat Controller to direct the helicopter in the dark night conditions. Bluebeard took off and began its hover. The dust its rotors kicked up, forced the Combat Controller to step backwards under the wing of a C-130 so he was better able to see. The pilot in Bluebeard 3 responded by moving forward as well, thinking he was drifting backward and the Combat Controller due to the dust, was his only reference point. In doing so, the RH-53D main rotor struck the EC-130's rear stabilizer. This caused the RH-53D to tip and then strike the wing root causing sparks which in turn ignited the now full wing tank. This lead to both the RH-53D and EC-130 bursting into flames that quickly engulfed both aircraft as the EC-130 was quickly evacuated. The ammunition started "cooking off," all the various missiles, grenades, explosives, and small arms rounds on both aircraft, causing loud, cracking explosions and throwing out bursts of flame. The Redeye missiles, then started to go off, creating smoke trails high into the sky. Finally the fuel bladders ignited, sending a huge column of flame skyward in a loud explosion that buckled the fuselage of the C-130. All four propellers dropped straight down into the sand still standing upright.

The men inside C-130, had felt the plane begin to shudder, as if the engines were being throttled up ready for take-off. The hold of the C-130 had no windows, so the men inside couldn't tell if they were moving yet. After the shudder, they heard two dull bangs as if the landing gear had hit a rock or a rut on the runway. One of the men Fitch looked towards the front of the plane only to see flames and sparks. The loadmaster had also seen flames licking their way around the hold and quickly opened the troop door on the port side of the plane. As he opened it, it revealed a wall of flame and the door was quickly shut. They tried the ramp and that too revealed flames, this meant their only way out was via the starboard troop door. The intense heat could already be felt in the hold - men started to leap out even before the door had been fully opened. The speed in which the fire spread was freighting. Men started piling out of it before it was completely open. Flames were spreading fast along the roof, then running down the walls on both sides, causing panic amongst the men. Inside the hold was a 1000 Gallon bladder full of aviation fuel that the flames had yet to reach. The initial explosion had blown a crew member from another C-130 some 100 feet away, clean off his feet. From his position he could see the RH-53D sat on top of the C-130 at a precarious angle engulfed in flames.

The exploding aircraft and ammunition sent flaming bits of hot metal and debris shooting out in all directions across the makeshift airport, riddling the four remaining working helicopters, whose crews jumped out and quickly moved to a safe distance. Most of the men had no idea what was going on; they knew only that a plane and a helicopter had been destroyed. The air over the scene was heavy with the smell of fuel and thick black smoke billowed up skywards. The remaining C-130s began taxiing in different directions away from the intense fire in fear of getting caught up in an even bigger explosion.

Five airmen from the USAF and the three USMC aircrew on the RH-53D all died in the ensuing conflagration. The intense fire reduced some of the bodies to little more than a pile of ash. The pilot and co-pilot, although badly burned, managed to survive the crash. They had jumped from their burning cockpit, hitting the ground quite hard adding to their injuries. It was a tragic loss of life all due to a pilot, following what he thought was the correct command. A shortage of fuel for the EC-130 to make it to its destination also played a part in the decision, on what would be a dangerous manoeuvre in clear conditions. At night with poor visibility made it an almost foolhardy manoeuvre, made worse with pilots that were not specifically trained to fly in such conditions.

There was no choice but to abort the mission; the President had now been made aware of the recommendation. The five RH-53Ds would have to be left behind and would later be put into active service in the Iranian air force, along with the six the Iranians already had. The 130s carried the remaining forces back to Masirah Island, which was being used as an intermediate airfield. Two C-141 medical evacuation aircraft were standing by. They picked up the injured personnel, Delta Force operatives, Rangers, helicopter crews and personnel. The CIA team also went away, unaware that they had been compromised.

America's elite rescue force had lost eight men, seven helicopters, and a C-130, and before it had even made contact with the enemy.

At 1am on the day after the failed attempt, the White House announced the failure of Operation Eagle Claw. The hostage takers, upon realising what had happened, decided to make any further attempt much more difficult by scattering the hostages across Iran. The people on Iranian bus that had been detained were able to give eyewitness accounts of the planned operation to the Iranian security forces.

Even though the first operation had failed, planning began in earnest for a second operation, called 'Project Honey Badger'. Plans and exercise were successfully undertaken, but due to the scattering of hostages, a battalion of soldiers would be required along with approximately 50 aircraft. Helicopters were felt to be too unreliable, so only fixed wing aircraft would be used. One development was the fitting of rockets fore and aft to a C-130 to create the YMC-130H that would allow for STOL (Short Take Off and Landing). The first fully modified aircraft undertook a demonstration flight at Duke Field at Eglin Air Force Base on 29 October 1980. During landing, it's landing brake rockets were fired too soon and caused a hard touchdown, which tore off the starboard wing and started a fire. The change of administration that was on the horizon meant the project was abandoned. Despite the failure of the YMC-130H, the 'Honey Badger' exercise continued until after the 1980 US election when Ronald Reagan became president.

One of the issues with the original operation was the inability of the various forces to work together cohesively, with each one having their own agenda. This led to the creation of a multi-service organisation called USSOCOM (United States Special Operations Command) several years later, which became operational in April 1987. Another issue was the lack of well-trained pilots that could operate at low level and night conditions in support of clandestine and Special Forces missions. This led to the creation of the 160th Special Operations Regiment, also called the Night Stalkers.

President Carter continued to try to secure the hostages' release before his term in office ended. Despite extensive last-negotiations, he did not succeed. Finally, on 20 January 1981, only a matter of minutes after President Carter's term had ended, the 52 US captives still being held in Iran were released, finally ending the 444-day Iran hostage crisis.

The Holloway report on Operation Eagle Claw laid out in detail the deficiencies of Special Forces aviation that had led to the mission disaster at Desert I. Chief among them was the lack of interoperability between the armed services. The conglomeration of hardware fielded by special operations aviation was the most apparent shortcoming. During the early 1980s, special operations aviation carried on with a wide variety of helicopters. Depending on the mission and what was available a Delta operative might find themselves in a CH-3 Jolly Green Giant, CH53C Sea Stallion, UH-1N twin Hueys, CH-47D Chinooks alongside newer and heavily modified UH-60 Blackhawks, H-53B and C Pave Low IIIs, and MH-6 Little Birds.

The Sea Stallions used in Eagle Claw were highly capable, but only amounted to 24 aircraft before half was lost at Dasht-e-Kavir. They were highly suitable for carrier operations as the blades folded fitted onto an aircraft carrier elevator without having to remove any blades as was the norm with many other helicopter types.

The Holloway report was on the whole agreed with and some organizational an equipment improvements were made. The 1987 Defense Authorization Act, established a unified command incorporating the Special Operations Forces from all services. The new Special Operations Command (SOCOM) could train and deploy throughout the world and was also given the authority to develop and acquire equipment, service and supplies unique to Special Forces operations. Delta's main interest was the authorization to modify existing aircraft and develop new helicopter variants that followed their mission profiles.

The UH-60 was reconfigured into three basic models to support all services. The Army's 160th Special Operations Aviation would use the H-60K Pav Hawk to replace the less capable MH-60As. For the assault role the HH-60H Rescue Hawk would enhance the Navy's search and rescue and Special Forces capability. The Air Force MH-60G Pave Hawk would replace both ageing search and rescue aircraft and act as an armed escort for the new MH-53J Pave Low IIs just entering service. All this aided Special Forces operations and continued development of aircraft such as the MH-6 and MH-47.

B Squadron which was one half of Delta had come within a millimeter of perishing in the Iranian desert. If that had happed one hell of a lot of hard-won institutional knowledge would have died right along with them. This gave Delta the impetus to write everything down to ensure that if anyone was killed following Delta had something to go on and learn from. One other important decision was to we design and then have made fire-resistant assault suits. B Squadron had almost burned to death. Historical studies shown that about 30 percent of combat casualties were the result of burns. So ever afterward, Delta would wear black suits on missions in the future. In fact, the suits Delta originally designed have become the ideal of SWAT teams around the world. Delta men are a pretty resilient bunch, and though no one likes to fail. They cinched up their morale, dusted ourselves off, and got ready for another attempt. At the upper command level, there was a fainthearted effort to plan a second operation to go after the hostages, but it was obvious to us that no one in Washington had their heart in the idea.

Made in the USA
Coppell, TX
07 February 2024

28736414R00059